50 Japan Premium Food Recipes for Home

By: Kelly Johnson

Table of Contents

- Wagyu Beef Shabu-Shabu
- Sukiyaki
- Chirashi Sushi
- Omakase Sushi
- Tempura Udon
- Kaiseki Bento Box
- Kobe Beef Steak
- Miso Ramen
- Unagi Donburi
- Yakiniku
- Okonomiyaki
- Takoyaki
- Katsu Curry
- Yuba (Tofu Skin) Salad
- Tonkotsu Ramen
- Ebi Fry (Fried Shrimp)
- Soba Noodles with Dipping Sauce
- Nabe (Hot Pot)
- Hiyayakko (Cold Tofu)
- Ebi Chili
- Miso Glazed Black Cod
- Japanese Style Fried Rice
- Gyudon (Beef Bowl)
- Chicken Teriyaki
- Spicy Tuna Don
- Zaru Soba (Chilled Soba Noodles)
- Shabu-Shabu Salad
- Japanese Cheesecake
- Matcha Tiramisu
- Mochi Ice Cream
- Kakigori (Shaved Ice)
- Red Bean Soup (Zenzai)

- Japanese Pumpkin Tempura
- Yakitori (Grilled Chicken Skewers)
- Shirasu (Whitebait) Rice Bowl
- Mentaiko Pasta
- Takoyaki Okonomiyaki
- Sukiyaki Beef Rolls
- Goya Champuru (Bitter Melon Stir-Fry)
- Tempura Soba
- Katsu Sandwich
- Yakimeshi (Fried Rice)
- Miso Soup with Clams
- Kake Udon
- Korean BBQ Beef
- Japanese Style Omelette (Tamagoyaki)
- Saba Misoni (Miso Braised Mackerel)
- Wasabi Mashed Potatoes
- Nasu Dengaku (Miso Grilled Eggplant)
- Shiro Ebi (White Shrimp) Tempura

Wagyu Beef Shabu-Shabu

Ingredients:

For the Broth:

- 4 cups dashi stock (you can use instant dashi or homemade)
- 2 cups water
- 2-3 tablespoons soy sauce
- 1 tablespoon mirin
- 1 tablespoon sake
- 1-2 tablespoons salt (to taste)

For the Shabu-Shabu:

- 1/2 pound Wagyu beef, thinly sliced (ensure slices are paper-thin for best results)
- 1 cup mushrooms (shiitake, enoki, or oyster mushrooms), sliced or whole
- 1 cup napa cabbage, cut into bite-sized pieces
- 1 cup spinach leaves or other leafy greens
- 1/2 cup tofu, cut into cubes
- 1 carrot, thinly sliced or cut into rounds
- 1-2 cups udon noodles or rice noodles (optional)

For the Dipping Sauces:

- **Ponzu Sauce:**
    - 1/4 cup soy sauce
    - 1/4 cup citrus juice (like yuzu or lemon)
    - 1 tablespoon mirin
    - 1 teaspoon sugar
- **Sesame Sauce:**
    - 1/4 cup tahini or sesame paste
    - 1 tablespoon soy sauce
    - 1 tablespoon rice vinegar
    - 1 tablespoon sugar
    - 1 teaspoon sesame oil
    - 1/4 cup water (to adjust consistency)

Instructions:

1. **Prepare the Broth**:
    - In a large pot, combine the dashi stock, water, soy sauce, mirin, sake, and salt. Bring to a simmer over medium heat.
2. **Prepare the Ingredients**:

        - Arrange the thinly sliced Wagyu beef, mushrooms, napa cabbage, spinach, tofu, and carrot on a large platter.
3. **Make the Dipping Sauces**:
    - For the **Ponzu Sauce**: In a small bowl, mix together the soy sauce, citrus juice, mirin, and sugar.
    - For the **Sesame Sauce**: In another bowl, combine the tahini or sesame paste, soy sauce, rice vinegar, sugar, sesame oil, and water. Adjust the water to reach your desired consistency.
4. **Cook the Shabu-Shabu**:
    - Place the pot of broth on a portable burner at the dining table to keep it hot. Bring the broth to a simmer.
    - Using chopsticks or a slotted spoon, cook the beef slices by dipping them briefly into the simmering broth (about 10-15 seconds) until they are just cooked through. Remove and dip into your choice of dipping sauce.
    - Add vegetables, tofu, and noodles to the broth as desired. Cook until the vegetables are tender and the tofu is heated through.
5. **Serve**:
    - Serve the cooked Wagyu beef and vegetables with the dipping sauces. Enjoy the hot pot style meal by dipping the cooked ingredients into the sauces and savoring the flavors.

Notes:

- **Wagyu Beef**: The thin slicing of the Wagyu beef is crucial for a quick cook time and tender texture. If you don't have access to Wagyu, you can use high-quality beef such as ribeye or sirloin.
- **Broth Flavor**: Adjust the seasoning of the broth to taste. You can add more soy sauce or salt if you prefer a stronger flavor.
- **Dipping Sauces**: The dipping sauces are essential for enhancing the flavor of the cooked ingredients. You can adjust the sweetness and tanginess according to your preference.
- **Additional Ingredients**: Feel free to add other vegetables or ingredients to the hot pot, such as bok choy, corn, or radish.

Wagyu Beef Shabu-Shabu is a wonderful way to enjoy the rich flavor of Wagyu beef in a social, interactive meal. The brief cooking time preserves the delicate texture of the beef, making it a luxurious and satisfying dish.

Sukiyaki

Ingredients:

For the Sukiyaki Sauce (Warishita):

- 1/2 cup soy sauce
- 1/2 cup mirin
- 1/2 cup sake
- 1/4 cup granulated sugar
- 1/2 cup dashi stock (you can use instant dashi or homemade)

For the Sukiyaki:

- 1/2 pound beef (sirloin or ribeye), thinly sliced
- 1 cup tofu, cut into cubes
- 1 cup mushrooms (shiitake, enoki, or oyster mushrooms), sliced or whole
- 1 cup napa cabbage, cut into bite-sized pieces
- 1 cup spinach leaves or other leafy greens
- 1-2 carrots, thinly sliced or cut into rounds
- 1-2 cups udon noodles or rice noodles (optional)
- 1 bunch green onions, cut into 2-inch pieces
- 1 tablespoon vegetable oil

For Serving:

- Cooked rice (optional)
- Raw egg (optional, for dipping)

Instructions:

1. **Prepare the Sukiyaki Sauce**:
    - In a bowl, mix together the soy sauce, mirin, sake, sugar, and dashi stock until the sugar is dissolved. Set aside.
2. **Prepare the Ingredients**:
    - Arrange the sliced beef, tofu, mushrooms, napa cabbage, spinach, carrots, and green onions on a large platter.
    - If using noodles, cook them according to package instructions and set aside.
3. **Heat the Pot**:
    - Heat a large, heavy-bottomed pot or a Japanese sukiyaki pot over medium heat. Add the vegetable oil and swirl to coat the bottom of the pot.
4. **Cook the Beef**:
    - Add the beef slices to the pot and cook until browned. You can add a little bit of the sukiyaki sauce to the beef as it cooks for extra flavor.

5. **Add the Sauce**:
   - Pour the sukiyaki sauce over the beef in the pot. Bring to a simmer.
6. **Add Vegetables and Tofu**:
   - Add the tofu, mushrooms, napa cabbage, spinach, carrots, and green onions to the pot. Simmer until the vegetables are tender and the tofu is heated through, about 5-10 minutes.
7. **Add Noodles** (if using):
   - If you are adding noodles, add them to the pot and cook until heated through.
8. **Serve**:
   - Ladle the Sukiyaki into bowls, making sure to include some of the broth with each serving. Serve with cooked rice if desired.
   - If you like, you can serve raw eggs on the side for dipping the cooked ingredients. To use, crack a raw egg into a small bowl and gently dip the hot ingredients into the egg before eating.

Notes:

- **Beef**: Thinly sliced beef is essential for Sukiyaki. You can ask your butcher to slice it for you or buy pre-sliced beef from an Asian grocery store.
- **Sauce Adjustments**: Feel free to adjust the sweetness and saltiness of the Sukiyaki sauce to your taste by adding more sugar or soy sauce as needed.
- **Vegetables**: You can use a variety of vegetables depending on what's in season or your personal preference. Common additions include mushrooms, bamboo shoots, and onions.
- **Raw Egg**: The raw egg is a traditional accompaniment that adds richness and helps mellow the flavors. However, it's optional and can be omitted if you prefer.

Sukiyaki is a wonderful dish for family gatherings or special occasions, offering a delicious, interactive dining experience where everyone can enjoy cooking and eating together.

Chirashi Sushi

Ingredients:

For the Sushi Rice:

- 2 cups sushi rice
- 2 1/2 cups water
- 1/2 cup rice vinegar
- 1/4 cup sugar
- 1 teaspoon salt

For the Toppings:

- 1/2 pound sushi-grade tuna, sliced into bite-sized pieces
- 1/2 pound sushi-grade salmon, sliced into bite-sized pieces
- 1/2 cup cooked shrimp, peeled and deveined
- 1/2 cup pickled ginger, sliced
- 1/2 cup thinly sliced cucumber
- 1/2 cup sliced avocado
- 1/4 cup thinly sliced radish
- 1/4 cup shredded nori (seaweed)
- 2 tablespoons soy sauce, for drizzling
- 1 tablespoon sesame seeds (optional)
- 1 tablespoon chopped fresh cilantro or green onions (optional)

For Garnish:

- Pickled vegetables (such as takuan or oshinko)
- Wasabi
- Additional soy sauce for dipping

Instructions:

1. **Prepare the Sushi Rice**:
   - Rinse the sushi rice under cold water until the water runs clear. This removes excess starch.
   - In a rice cooker or a pot, combine the rinsed rice with 2 1/2 cups of water. Cook according to the rice cooker instructions or bring to a boil, then reduce heat to low, cover, and simmer for 18-20 minutes until the water is absorbed and the rice is tender. Remove from heat and let it sit covered for 10 minutes.
   - While the rice is cooking, in a small saucepan, heat the rice vinegar, sugar, and salt over low heat, stirring until the sugar and salt dissolve. Do not boil.

        - Transfer the cooked rice to a large bowl and gently fold in the vinegar mixture. Let the rice cool to room temperature.
  2. **Prepare the Toppings**:
        - Arrange the sushi-grade tuna and salmon slices, cooked shrimp, pickled ginger, cucumber, avocado, and radish on a serving platter or individual bowls.
  3. **Assemble the Chirashi Sushi**:
        - Divide the sushi rice among bowls or plates. Gently spread the rice out.
        - Top the rice with the assorted ingredients: tuna, salmon, shrimp, cucumber, avocado, radish, and pickled ginger.
  4. **Garnish**:
        - Sprinkle with shredded nori, sesame seeds, and chopped cilantro or green onions if desired.
        - Drizzle a little soy sauce over the top or serve on the side.
  5. **Serve**:
        - Serve immediately with pickled vegetables, wasabi, and additional soy sauce for dipping.

Notes:

- **Sushi Rice**: Sushi rice is essential for authentic Chirashi Sushi. If you don't have a rice cooker, you can use a pot with a tight-fitting lid to cook the rice.
- **Fresh Ingredients**: Use high-quality, sushi-grade fish and seafood for the best flavor and safety. You can substitute or add other ingredients such as crab, eel, or pickled radish according to your preference.
- **Rice Vinegar Mixture**: The vinegar mixture should be added to the rice while it's still warm to help the flavors meld.
- **Customization**: Chirashi Sushi is highly customizable. Feel free to adjust the toppings based on seasonal ingredients or personal preferences.

Chirashi Sushi is a beautiful and versatile dish that allows you to enjoy a variety of fresh flavors and textures in a single bowl. It's perfect for entertaining or a special treat!

Omakase Sushi

1. Preparation

- **Ingredients**: Use high-quality, sushi-grade fish and seafood. Freshness is key.
- **Equipment**: Sharp knife, sushi mat, and a rice cooker or pot.

2. Sushi Rice Recipe

Ingredients:

- 2 cups sushi rice
- 2 1/2 cups water
- 1/2 cup rice vinegar
- 1/4 cup sugar
- 1 teaspoon salt

Instructions:

1. Rinse sushi rice under cold water until the water runs clear.
2. Cook rice according to the rice cooker or pot instructions.
3. Heat vinegar, sugar, and salt in a saucepan until dissolved. Do not boil.
4. Gently fold the vinegar mixture into the cooked rice. Allow it to cool to room temperature.

3. Omakase Sushi Selection

1. Maguro (Tuna) Nigiri

- Slice sushi-grade tuna into small, thin pieces.
- Form small balls of sushi rice and top with a slice of tuna.
- Optionally, add a touch of wasabi between the rice and tuna.

2. Salmon (Sake) Nigiri

- Slice sushi-grade salmon into thin pieces.
- Form sushi rice balls and top with a slice of salmon.
- Garnish with a small amount of soy sauce or a touch of lemon zest.

3. Ebi (Shrimp) Nigiri

- Boil or steam shrimp until cooked and cool.
- Peel and devein shrimp, then place on top of a sushi rice ball.

4. Unagi (Grilled Eel) Nigiri

- Grill or pan-sear eel until cooked and glazed with eel sauce.
- Slice eel and place on top of sushi rice.
- Drizzle with additional eel sauce if desired.

**5. Tamago (Sweet Egg Omelet) Nigiri

- Make a tamago omelet by whisking eggs, sugar, and soy sauce, then cook in a pan until set.
- Slice the omelet into thin pieces and place on sushi rice.

**6. Toro (Fatty Tuna) Nigiri

- Slice fatty tuna into thin pieces.
- Top sushi rice with a slice of toro.
- Add a touch of sea salt or a small drop of soy sauce.

**7. Ikura (Salmon Roe) Nigiri

- Spoon salmon roe over sushi rice.
- Garnish with a touch of chives or scallions.

**8. Miso Soup

- Prepare a traditional miso soup with dashi broth and miso paste.
- Add tofu cubes and seaweed.

**9. Pickled Vegetables

- Serve with assorted pickled vegetables such as pickled ginger, daikon radish, or cucumbers.

4. Presentation

- **Plating**: Arrange the nigiri and other sushi on a sushi platter or individual plates.
- **Garnishes**: Include garnishes such as pickled ginger, wasabi, and soy sauce for dipping.

5. Serving

- **Accompaniments**: Serve with miso soup and pickled vegetables on the side.
- **Dipping Sauces**: Provide soy sauce and wasabi for additional flavor.

Notes:

- **Fish Freshness**: Ensure all fish and seafood are sushi-grade for safety and the best taste.
- **Rice Texture**: Sushi rice should be slightly sticky but not mushy.

- **Customizing**: Feel free to add other sushi types or variations, such as maki rolls or sashimi.

Creating an Omakase Sushi experience at home is a way to showcase your skills and offer a luxurious meal, with attention to detail and quality ingredients. Enjoy the process of preparing and serving a variety of fresh and flavorful sushi dishes!

Tempura Udon

Ingredients:

For the Udon Soup:

- 4 cups dashi stock (can use instant dashi or homemade)
- 1/4 cup soy sauce
- 1/4 cup mirin
- 2 tablespoons sake
- 1 tablespoon sugar
- 2 green onions, sliced (for garnish)
- 1 tablespoon sesame oil (optional, for added flavor)

For the Tempura:

- **Tempura Batter:**
    - 1 cup all-purpose flour
    - 1 large egg
    - 1 cup ice-cold sparkling water (or cold water)
    - 1/2 teaspoon baking powder (optional, for extra crispiness)
- **Tempura Ingredients:**
    - 8-10 shrimp, peeled and deveined
    - 1 cup sweet potato, thinly sliced
    - 1 cup zucchini, thinly sliced
    - 1 cup mushrooms (shiitake, enoki, or oyster), whole or sliced
    - 1/2 cup cornstarch (for dusting)
    - Vegetable oil (for frying)

For Garnish:

- 2 green onions, sliced
- Pickled ginger (optional)
- Seaweed (nori), shredded (optional)
- Shredded daikon radish (optional)

Instructions:

1. **Prepare the Tempura Batter:**
    - In a bowl, whisk together the flour and baking powder.
    - In another bowl, beat the egg and add the ice-cold sparkling water. Mix well.
    - Gently fold the wet ingredients into the dry ingredients. Be careful not to overmix; the batter should be lumpy.
2. **Prepare the Tempura:**

- Heat vegetable oil in a deep pan or fryer to 350°F (180°C).
- Lightly dust the shrimp, sweet potato, zucchini, and mushrooms with cornstarch. This helps the batter stick better.
- Dip the vegetables and shrimp into the tempura batter, allowing excess batter to drip off.
- Carefully place the battered ingredients into the hot oil and fry until golden brown and crispy, about 2-4 minutes per batch.
- Remove with a slotted spoon and drain on paper towels. Keep warm.
3. **Prepare the Udon Soup:**
    - In a large pot, combine the dashi stock, soy sauce, mirin, sake, and sugar. Bring to a simmer over medium heat.
    - Taste the broth and adjust seasoning if needed.
4. **Cook the Udon Noodles:**
    - Cook udon noodles according to the package instructions. Drain and rinse under cold water to stop cooking.
5. **Assemble the Dish:**
    - Divide the cooked udon noodles among bowls.
    - Ladle the hot broth over the noodles.
    - Top each bowl with pieces of tempura.
    - Garnish with sliced green onions, pickled ginger, shredded nori, and shredded daikon radish if using.
6. **Serve:**
    - Serve immediately while hot.

Notes:

- **Dashi Stock**: Dashi is a fundamental component of Japanese cuisine. You can use instant dashi for convenience or make your own from kombu (sea kelp) and bonito flakes.
- **Tempura**: Ensure the oil is hot enough to get a crispy texture. If the oil is too cool, the tempura will be greasy and not as crisp.
- **Noodles**: Udon noodles can be purchased fresh, frozen, or dried. Follow the cooking instructions on the package for best results.
- **Garnishes**: Customize your toppings based on your preferences or what's available. Some additional options include tempura vegetables or mushrooms.

Tempura Udon is a satisfying and flavorful dish that combines the richness of tempura with the comforting qualities of a hot noodle soup. Enjoy preparing and savoring this classic Japanese comfort food!

Kaiseki Bento Box

Components:

1. **Rice Dish**
2. **Protein Dish**
3. **Vegetable Dish**
4. **Pickles**
5. **Soup or Stew**
6. **Fruit or Dessert**

Recipe Components:

1. Rice Dish: Teriyaki Chicken Rice

Ingredients:

- 2 boneless, skinless chicken thighs
- 1/4 cup soy sauce
- 2 tablespoons mirin
- 2 tablespoons sake
- 2 tablespoons brown sugar
- 1 tablespoon vegetable oil
- 2 cups cooked white rice

Instructions:

1. **Prepare the Teriyaki Sauce:**
   - In a small bowl, mix soy sauce, mirin, sake, and brown sugar until the sugar dissolves.
2. **Cook the Chicken:**
   - Heat vegetable oil in a pan over medium heat. Add chicken thighs and cook until browned on both sides, about 5-7 minutes per side.
   - Pour the teriyaki sauce over the chicken and simmer until the chicken is cooked through and the sauce thickens, about 10 minutes.
   - Slice the chicken into bite-sized pieces and serve over cooked rice.

2. Protein Dish: Grilled Salmon with Miso Glaze

Ingredients:

- 2 salmon fillets
- 1/4 cup miso paste
- 2 tablespoons soy sauce

- 2 tablespoons mirin
- 1 tablespoon sugar

Instructions:

1. **Prepare the Miso Glaze:**
   - In a bowl, mix miso paste, soy sauce, mirin, and sugar until smooth.
2. **Grill the Salmon:**
   - Preheat a grill or broiler. Brush salmon fillets with the miso glaze and grill or broil for 4-6 minutes per side, until cooked through and slightly charred.

3. Vegetable Dish: Steamed Broccoli and Carrots

Ingredients:

- 1 cup broccoli florets
- 1 cup carrot slices
- Salt and pepper to taste

Instructions:

1. **Steam the Vegetables:**
   - Steam broccoli and carrots until tender, about 5-7 minutes. Season with salt and pepper.

4. Pickles: Japanese Pickled Radish (Takuan)

Ingredients:

- 1 daikon radish, peeled and sliced
- 1/4 cup rice vinegar
- 1/4 cup sugar
- 1/4 cup salt

Instructions:

1. **Pickle the Radish:**
   - In a bowl, mix rice vinegar, sugar, and salt until the sugar and salt dissolve.
   - Add radish slices and let sit for at least 30 minutes, or refrigerate for longer pickling.

5. Soup: Miso Soup

Ingredients:

- 4 cups dashi stock
- 1/4 cup miso paste

- 1/2 cup tofu, cubed
- 1/4 cup sliced green onions
- 1/4 cup seaweed (wakame), rehydrated

Instructions:

1. **Prepare the Miso Soup:**
   - Heat dashi stock in a pot until warm.
   - Dissolve miso paste in a small amount of hot dashi and then add it back to the pot.
   - Add tofu and seaweed. Heat gently without boiling.
   - Garnish with sliced green onions before serving.

6. Dessert: Fresh Fruit or Sweet Red Bean Paste

Option 1: Fresh Fruit

- Sliced seasonal fruit such as melon, apple, or berries.

Option 2: Sweet Red Bean Paste (Anko)

- 1 cup red beans
- 1 cup sugar
- 1 cup water

Instructions for Anko:

1. **Prepare the Red Beans:**
   - Cook beans in water until soft, then drain.
   - In a pot, combine beans and sugar with water. Simmer until thickened.
   - Cool before using.

Assembling the Bento Box:

1. **Layer the Components:**
   - Use a bento box or similar container with separate compartments.
   - Arrange the rice dish in one section, the grilled salmon in another, and the steamed vegetables in another.
   - Place the pickles in a small section.
   - Include a small bowl or container for the miso soup.
   - Add a portion of fresh fruit or a small serving of sweet red bean paste for dessert.
2. **Garnish:**
   - Garnish with a sprig of parsley or a few sesame seeds for extra flair.

Notes:

- **Presentation**: In Kaiseki, presentation is as important as flavor. Arrange the food attractively and use a variety of colors and textures.
- **Customization**: Feel free to adjust the ingredients based on personal preferences or seasonal availability.
- **Seasonality**: Kaiseki emphasizes seasonal ingredients, so adapt the bento box to highlight the best of each season.

Creating a Kaiseki Bento Box is a wonderful way to enjoy a range of flavors and textures, all presented in a beautifully arranged and balanced meal. Enjoy your culinary experience!

Kobe Beef Steak

Ingredients:

- 2 Kobe beef steaks (about 6-8 ounces each, 1-1.5 inches thick)
- Salt, to taste
- Freshly ground black pepper, to taste
- 1 tablespoon vegetable oil (or any high-heat cooking oil)
- 2 tablespoons unsalted butter (optional, for finishing)

For Serving (Optional):

- Soy sauce
- Wasabi
- Pickled ginger
- Steamed vegetables
- Rice or mashed potatoes

Instructions:

1. **Prepare the Steak:**
    - Remove the Kobe beef steaks from the refrigerator about 30 minutes before cooking to allow them to come to room temperature. This ensures even cooking.
2. **Season the Steak:**
    - Just before cooking, season the steaks generously with salt and freshly ground black pepper.
3. **Preheat the Pan:**
    - Heat a heavy-bottomed skillet or cast-iron pan over medium-high heat. If you're using a grill, preheat it to high heat.
4. **Cook the Steak:**
    - Add vegetable oil to the hot skillet and swirl to coat.
    - Place the steaks in the pan and cook for 2-3 minutes on each side for medium-rare, or until a golden-brown crust forms. Adjust the time based on your preferred doneness.
        - **Rare**: 1-2 minutes per side
        - **Medium-Rare**: 2-3 minutes per side
        - **Medium**: 3-4 minutes per side
        - **Medium-Well**: 4-5 minutes per side
        - **Well-Done**: 5-6 minutes per side
5. **Optional Butter Finish:**
    - If desired, add a tablespoon of unsalted butter to the pan during the last minute of cooking. Baste the steaks with the melted butter for extra richness.
6. **Rest the Steak:**

- Remove the steaks from the pan and let them rest on a cutting board for about 5 minutes. This allows the juices to redistribute, ensuring a tender and juicy steak.
7. **Slice and Serve:**
    - Slice the steak against the grain to maintain tenderness.
    - Serve with your choice of side dishes, such as steamed vegetables, rice, or mashed potatoes. You can also offer soy sauce, wasabi, and pickled ginger on the side.

Notes:

- **Pan Temperature**: Ensure the pan or grill is hot before adding the steaks to get a good sear.
- **Doneness**: Kobe beef is best enjoyed medium-rare to medium, as overcooking can diminish its rich flavor and tenderness.
- **Resting**: Allowing the steak to rest is crucial for keeping it juicy. Don't skip this step.
- **Accompaniments**: Simple sides complement the richness of Kobe beef. Avoid overpowering sauces; a light soy sauce or a touch of wasabi can enhance the flavor without overshadowing it.

Kobe beef steak is a true luxury, celebrated for its exceptional quality. By following these guidelines, you can enjoy a perfectly cooked Kobe steak that highlights its unique characteristics.

Miso Ramen

Ingredients:

For the Broth:

- 4 cups chicken or vegetable broth
- 1 cup water
- 1/4 cup miso paste (white or red, depending on your preference)
- 2 tablespoons soy sauce
- 1 tablespoon sesame oil
- 2 garlic cloves, minced
- 1-inch piece of ginger, peeled and minced
- 1 tablespoon vegetable oil

For the Ramen:

- 4 oz dried or fresh ramen noodles
- 1 cup sliced mushrooms (shiitake, button, or your choice)
- 1 cup baby spinach or bok choy
- 1 cup corn kernels (fresh or frozen)
- 1/2 cup sliced green onions
- 2 large eggs
- 1 tablespoon sesame seeds (for garnish)
- 1 sheet nori (seaweed), cut into strips (optional)

For Toppings (Optional):

- Sliced cooked chicken, pork, or tofu
- Bean sprouts
- Bamboo shoots
- Sliced chili peppers or chili oil

Instructions:

1. **Prepare the Broth:**
   - Heat vegetable oil in a large pot over medium heat. Add minced garlic and ginger, and sauté until fragrant, about 1-2 minutes.
   - Add chicken or vegetable broth and water to the pot. Bring to a simmer.
   - In a small bowl, whisk together miso paste and a few spoonfuls of hot broth until smooth. Stir the miso mixture back into the pot.
   - Add soy sauce and sesame oil. Stir to combine. Simmer for 10 minutes to allow flavors to meld. Adjust seasoning if needed.
2. **Cook the Noodles:**

- In a separate pot, cook ramen noodles according to the package instructions. Drain and rinse under cold water to stop cooking. Set aside.

3. **Prepare the Toppings:**
   - **Mushrooms:** Sauté mushrooms in a bit of oil until tender, about 5 minutes.
   - **Corn:** If using frozen corn, thaw and heat briefly.
   - **Spinach or Bok Choy:** Quickly blanch in boiling water for 1-2 minutes if desired.
   - **Eggs:** Soft-boil eggs by placing them in boiling water for 6-7 minutes. Transfer to an ice bath to cool, then peel and set aside.

4. **Assemble the Ramen:**
   - Divide cooked noodles between bowls.
   - Pour the hot miso broth over the noodles.
   - Top with sautéed mushrooms, corn, spinach or bok choy, and sliced green onions.
   - Halve the soft-boiled eggs and place on top of each bowl.
   - Garnish with sesame seeds, nori strips, and any additional toppings like sliced chili peppers or bean sprouts.

5. **Serve:**
   - Serve immediately while hot. Enjoy your homemade miso ramen!

Notes:

- **Miso Paste:** White miso is milder and sweeter, while red miso has a stronger, more robust flavor. You can use either or a combination depending on your taste preference.
- **Broth Depth:** For a deeper flavor, you can add a splash of sake or a bit of miso tare (a concentrated miso mixture).
- **Customizations:** Feel free to customize the toppings based on what you have on hand or your personal preferences.

Miso ramen is a versatile and flavorful dish that's perfect for a cozy meal. Enjoy the process of making this classic Japanese comfort food at home!

Unagi Donburi

Ingredients:

For the Unagi:

- 2 eel fillets (unagi), pre-cooked or grilled (available at Asian markets)
- 1/4 cup soy sauce
- 1/4 cup mirin
- 2 tablespoons sugar
- 1/4 cup sake (optional)

For the Rice:

- 2 cups sushi or short-grain rice
- 2 1/2 cups water

For Garnish (Optional):

- Sliced green onions
- Shredded nori (seaweed)
- Pickled ginger

Instructions:

1. **Prepare the Rice:**
   - Rinse the rice under cold water until the water runs clear to remove excess starch.
   - In a rice cooker or a pot, combine the rinsed rice with 2 1/2 cups of water. Cook according to the rice cooker instructions or bring to a boil, then reduce heat to low, cover, and simmer for about 18 minutes. Let it sit for 10 minutes before fluffing with a fork.
2. **Prepare the Tare Sauce:**
   - In a small saucepan, combine soy sauce, mirin, sugar, and sake (if using).
   - Bring to a simmer over medium heat, stirring occasionally until the sugar dissolves and the sauce slightly thickens, about 5-7 minutes. Set aside.
3. **Prepare the Unagi:**
   - If using pre-cooked eel, remove it from the packaging and cut into serving-sized pieces.
   - If the eel needs to be grilled or reheated, preheat your grill or oven. Brush the eel with some of the tare sauce and grill for 2-3 minutes per side, or until warmed through and slightly caramelized. You can also use a broiler for this step.
4. **Assemble the Donburi:**
   - Divide the cooked rice into bowls.

- Place the grilled eel pieces on top of the rice.
- Brush additional tare sauce over the eel for extra flavor.

5. **Garnish and Serve:**
    - Garnish with sliced green onions, shredded nori, and pickled ginger if desired.
    - Serve immediately while hot.

Notes:

- **Eel Preparation:** Unagi fillets can often be found pre-cooked and glazed in Japanese grocery stores or online. If you purchase unagi that is not pre-cooked, you'll need to grill it yourself after preparing the tare sauce.
- **Tare Sauce:** Adjust the sweetness and saltiness of the tare sauce to your preference. You can make it ahead of time and store it in the refrigerator for up to a week.
- **Rice:** Sushi rice or short-grain rice is best for this dish as it is sticky and holds together well. If you use a different type of rice, you might need to adjust the cooking time and water amount.

Unagi Donburi is a rich and flavorful dish that highlights the unique taste of grilled eel with a sweet and savory glaze. Enjoy this classic Japanese comfort food as a satisfying meal any time!

Yakiniku

Ingredients:

For the Marinade:

- 1/4 cup soy sauce
- 2 tablespoons mirin
- 2 tablespoons sake
- 2 tablespoons sugar
- 2 garlic cloves, minced
- 1-inch piece of ginger, peeled and minced
- 1 tablespoon sesame oil
- 1 tablespoon grated pear (optional, for sweetness and tenderness)

For the Meat:

- 1 lb beef sirloin or ribeye, thinly sliced (or pork belly, chicken thighs, or your choice)
- 1-2 bell peppers, sliced
- 1 onion, sliced
- 1 cup mushrooms (shiitake, button, or your choice), sliced
- 1 zucchini, sliced
- 1 cup broccoli florets

For Dipping Sauce (Tare):

- 1/4 cup soy sauce
- 2 tablespoons mirin
- 2 tablespoons sake
- 1 tablespoon sugar
- 1 tablespoon grated garlic
- 1 tablespoon grated ginger

For Garnish (Optional):

- Sesame seeds
- Sliced green onions
- Shredded nori (seaweed)

Instructions:

1. **Prepare the Marinade:**
    - In a bowl, combine soy sauce, mirin, sake, sugar, minced garlic, minced ginger, sesame oil, and grated pear (if using). Stir until the sugar is dissolved.

2. **Marinate the Meat:**
   - Place the thinly sliced meat in a shallow dish or a resealable plastic bag. Pour the marinade over the meat, ensuring it is well-coated.
   - Marinate in the refrigerator for at least 30 minutes to 2 hours, or overnight for more flavor.
3. **Prepare the Vegetables:**
   - Slice the bell peppers, onion, mushrooms, zucchini, and broccoli.
4. **Prepare the Dipping Sauce (Tare):**
   - In a small bowl, combine soy sauce, mirin, sake, sugar, grated garlic, and grated ginger. Stir until the sugar is dissolved. Adjust seasoning to taste.
5. **Grill the Yakiniku:**
   - Preheat a grill or a grill pan over medium-high heat. If using a tabletop grill, heat it according to the manufacturer's instructions.
   - Grill the marinated meat and vegetables in batches, cooking each piece until it is nicely charred and cooked through. Thinly sliced meat will cook quickly, about 1-2 minutes per side.
   - For vegetables, grill until tender and slightly charred, about 3-5 minutes.
6. **Serve:**
   - Arrange the grilled meat and vegetables on a serving platter.
   - Serve with the dipping sauce (tare) on the side.
   - Garnish with sesame seeds, sliced green onions, and shredded nori if desired.

Notes:

- **Meat Choice:** Yakiniku traditionally uses beef, but you can use pork, chicken, or even seafood. Thin slices work best for quick grilling.
- **Marinade:** The marinade adds flavor and tenderness to the meat. For a more intense flavor, marinate the meat overnight.
- **Grilling:** If using a grill pan, make sure it is well-heated to get a good sear. Avoid overcrowding the pan to ensure even grilling.
- **Accompaniments:** Yakiniku is often enjoyed with steamed rice, pickled vegetables, and a simple salad. You can also serve it with a bowl of miso soup for a complete meal.

Yakiniku is a delightful way to enjoy a variety of grilled meats and vegetables with family and friends. Enjoy the interactive experience of grilling and savoring deliciously flavored meat and veggies right at your table!

Okonomiyaki

Ingredients:

For the Batter:

- 1 cup all-purpose flour
- 1 cup dashi stock (or water)
- 2 large eggs
- 1/4 teaspoon salt
- 1/4 teaspoon baking powder (optional, for extra fluffiness)

For the Filling:

- 2 cups shredded cabbage
- 1/2 cup thinly sliced green onions
- 1/2 cup grated carrot (optional)
- 1/2 cup cooked bacon or pork belly, chopped (or other preferred meat or seafood)
- 1/2 cup cooked shrimp or squid (optional)
- 1/4 cup pickled ginger, chopped (optional)

For Toppings:

- Okonomiyaki sauce (or a mix of Worcestershire sauce and ketchup)
- Japanese mayonnaise
- Bonito flakes (katsuobushi)
- Aonori (dried seaweed flakes)
- Sliced green onions

Instructions:

1. **Prepare the Batter:**
   - In a large bowl, whisk together the flour, dashi stock, eggs, salt, and baking powder until smooth. The batter should be thick but pourable.
2. **Add the Filling:**
   - Gently fold the shredded cabbage, green onions, grated carrot (if using), cooked bacon or pork belly, cooked shrimp or squid (if using), and pickled ginger (if using) into the batter. Mix until evenly combined.
3. **Preheat the Pan:**
   - Heat a large non-stick skillet or griddle over medium heat. Lightly oil the surface with vegetable oil or cooking spray.
4. **Cook the Okonomiyaki:**

- Pour a portion of the batter onto the skillet and spread it into a thick pancake, about 1/2 inch to 1 inch thick. Use a spatula to shape it into a round or oval shape.
- Cook for about 4-5 minutes on the first side, until the bottom is golden brown and crispy. Flip carefully using two spatulas or by sliding it onto a plate and flipping it.
- Cook the other side for another 4-5 minutes, until it is golden brown and the pancake is cooked through.

5. **Add Toppings:**
   - Transfer the cooked okonomiyaki to a serving plate. Drizzle with okonomiyaki sauce and Japanese mayonnaise.
   - Sprinkle with bonito flakes and aonori. Add sliced green onions for extra freshness.

6. **Serve:**
   - Cut into wedges and serve immediately while hot.

Notes:

- **Okonomiyaki Sauce:** If you can't find okonomiyaki sauce, a mix of Worcestershire sauce and ketchup works as a substitute. Some recipes also include soy sauce and a bit of honey for sweetness.
- **Customization:** Feel free to experiment with different fillings and toppings based on your preferences. Common variations include adding cheese, mushrooms, or different types of seafood.
- **Cooking Tips:** Ensure the skillet is properly heated before adding the batter to get a nice crispy texture. Don't overcrowd the skillet; cook in batches if necessary.
- **Serving Ideas:** Okonomiyaki is great on its own but can also be served with a side of miso soup or a light salad for a complete meal.

Enjoy making and eating this versatile and delicious Japanese savory pancake!

Takoyaki

Ingredients:

For the Takoyaki Batter:

- 1 cup all-purpose flour
- 1 1/2 cups dashi stock (or water)
- 2 large eggs
- 1/2 teaspoon baking powder
- 1/2 teaspoon soy sauce
- 1/2 teaspoon salt

For the Filling:

- 1/2 cup cooked octopus, diced (you can use pre-cooked octopus or boiled octopus)
- 1/4 cup tempura scraps (tenkasu)
- 2 tablespoons pickled ginger, finely chopped
- 2-3 green onions, finely chopped

For Toppings:

- Takoyaki sauce (store-bought or homemade)
- Japanese mayonnaise
- Aonori (dried seaweed flakes)
- Bonito flakes (katsuobushi)
- Sliced green onions

For Cooking:

- Vegetable oil (for greasing the takoyaki pan)

Instructions:

1. **Prepare the Takoyaki Batter:**
   - In a large bowl, whisk together the flour, dashi stock, eggs, baking powder, soy sauce, and salt until smooth and well combined.
2. **Prepare the Filling:**
   - Dice the cooked octopus into small, bite-sized pieces.
   - Prepare the tempura scraps, pickled ginger, and green onions.
3. **Preheat the Takoyaki Pan:**
   - Heat a takoyaki pan or an electric takoyaki grill over medium heat. If you don't have a takoyaki pan, you can use a regular muffin tin or pancake mold, but the traditional takoyaki pan with rounded molds is preferred.

4. **Oil the Pan:**
   - Brush the takoyaki pan with vegetable oil to prevent sticking. Make sure each mold is well-oiled.
5. **Cook the Takoyaki:**
   - Pour the batter into each mold, filling them to the top.
   - Add a small amount of diced octopus, tempura scraps, pickled ginger, and green onions into each mold.
   - Allow the batter to cook for about 2 minutes. As the edges start to set, use a takoyaki pick or chopsticks to gently turn the balls, so the uncooked batter flows into the mold and creates a round shape. Turn them frequently to ensure even cooking and a golden brown exterior. This may take around 4-5 minutes in total.
6. **Serve the Takoyaki:**
   - Once the takoyaki balls are evenly cooked and golden brown, remove them from the pan and transfer them to a serving plate.
   - Drizzle with takoyaki sauce and Japanese mayonnaise.
   - Sprinkle with aonori, bonito flakes, and additional sliced green onions if desired.
7. **Enjoy:**
   - Serve the takoyaki immediately while they're hot and crispy.

Notes:

- **Octopus:** If you can't find octopus, you can substitute with cooked shrimp or chicken, though it will change the traditional flavor of the dish.
- **Takoyaki Pan:** If you don't have a takoyaki pan, a cast-iron mini muffin tin or a silicone mold can be used, though the results might vary slightly.
- **Toppings:** Customize the toppings based on your preference. Takoyaki sauce and Japanese mayonnaise are essential for authentic flavor.
- **Cooking Tip:** Turning the takoyaki balls can be tricky. Using a takoyaki pick or chopsticks is essential for creating a perfectly round shape. Be patient and turn them carefully to get that signature texture.

Takoyaki is a fun and delicious dish to make and enjoy, especially for gatherings or as a tasty snack. Enjoy your homemade takoyaki with family and friends!

Katsu Curry

Ingredients:

For the Katsu:

- 4 boneless pork chops (about 1/2 inch thick)
- Salt and pepper, to taste
- 1/2 cup all-purpose flour
- 2 large eggs, beaten
- 1 cup panko breadcrumbs
- Vegetable oil, for frying

For the Curry Sauce:

- 1 tablespoon vegetable oil
- 1 onion, finely chopped
- 2 garlic cloves, minced
- 1-inch piece of ginger, peeled and minced
- 2 carrots, peeled and sliced
- 1 large potato, peeled and cubed
- 2 tablespoons curry powder (Japanese curry powder is preferred, but regular curry powder can be used)
- 2 tablespoons all-purpose flour
- 2 cups chicken or vegetable broth
- 1 tablespoon soy sauce
- 1 tablespoon Worcestershire sauce
- 1 tablespoon honey or sugar
- 1/2 cup frozen peas (optional)

For Serving:

- Steamed white rice
- Pickled ginger (optional)
- Chopped green onions (optional)

Instructions:

1. **Prepare the Pork Katsu:**
   - **Pound the Pork:** Lightly pound the pork chops between sheets of plastic wrap to an even thickness, about 1/2 inch thick. Season with salt and pepper.
   - **Bread the Pork:** Set up a breading station with three shallow dishes. Place flour in the first dish, beaten eggs in the second dish, and panko breadcrumbs in the third dish.

- Dredge each pork chop in flour, shaking off excess, then dip in the beaten eggs, and finally coat with panko breadcrumbs, pressing gently to adhere.

2. **Fry the Katsu:**
    - Heat about 1/2 inch of vegetable oil in a large skillet over medium heat.
    - Fry the breaded pork chops until golden brown and crispy, about 4-5 minutes per side. The internal temperature should reach 145°F (63°C). Adjust the heat as needed to avoid burning the breadcrumbs.
    - Remove the pork chops from the skillet and drain on paper towels. Let rest while you prepare the curry sauce.

3. **Prepare the Curry Sauce:**
    - **Sauté Aromatics:** In the same skillet, remove excess oil, leaving about 1 tablespoon. Add vegetable oil and heat over medium heat. Sauté onions until softened and translucent, about 5 minutes.
    - Add garlic and ginger, and cook for an additional 1-2 minutes until fragrant.
    - **Cook Vegetables:** Add carrots and potatoes to the skillet, and cook for 5 minutes, stirring occasionally.
    - **Add Curry Powder:** Stir in curry powder and flour, cooking for 1-2 minutes to toast the spices and flour.
    - **Add Broth:** Gradually add the chicken or vegetable broth while stirring to avoid lumps. Bring to a simmer and cook until vegetables are tender, about 15-20 minutes.
    - **Season:** Stir in soy sauce, Worcestershire sauce, and honey or sugar. Adjust seasoning as needed. If using, add frozen peas in the last few minutes of cooking.

4. **Serve:**
    - Slice the cooked katsu into strips.
    - Serve the curry sauce over steamed rice, and top with sliced katsu.
    - Garnish with pickled ginger and chopped green onions if desired.

Notes:

- **Katsu Variations:** You can substitute pork with chicken for a Chicken Katsu Curry. The preparation method remains the same.
- **Curry Sauce:** Japanese curry roux blocks can be used as a shortcut. Simply follow the package instructions and add vegetables and meat as desired.
- **Rice:** Steamed white rice is traditional, but you can also use brown rice or other types of rice if you prefer.
- **Vegetables:** Feel free to add other vegetables like bell peppers, mushrooms, or zucchini to the curry sauce based on your preference.

Katsu Curry is a delicious, comforting meal that combines crispy pork with a rich curry sauce, making it a favorite for many. Enjoy preparing and eating this flavorful Japanese dish!

Yuba (Tofu Skin) Salad

Ingredients:

For the Salad:

- 1 cup dried yuba (tofu skin) or fresh yuba if available
- 1 cup mixed salad greens (such as lettuce, arugula, or spinach)
- 1 cup shredded carrots
- 1/2 cup thinly sliced cucumber
- 1/2 cup cherry tomatoes, halved
- 1/4 cup thinly sliced radishes
- 1/4 cup sliced red bell pepper
- 1/4 cup chopped fresh cilantro or parsley (optional)

For the Dressing:

- 3 tablespoons soy sauce
- 2 tablespoons rice vinegar
- 1 tablespoon sesame oil
- 1 tablespoon honey or maple syrup
- 1 teaspoon grated ginger
- 1 clove garlic, minced
- 1 teaspoon toasted sesame seeds
- 1 teaspoon chili flakes (optional, for a bit of heat)

Instructions:

1. **Prepare the Yuba:**
   - **Dried Yuba:** If using dried yuba, soak it in warm water for 30 minutes or until soft and pliable. Drain and gently squeeze out excess water. If needed, cut into bite-sized strips or pieces.
   - **Fresh Yuba:** If using fresh yuba, simply cut it into bite-sized pieces or strips.
2. **Prepare the Salad Ingredients:**
   - Wash and prepare all salad vegetables as described: shred the carrots, slice the cucumber, halve the cherry tomatoes, slice the radishes and bell pepper. Chop the fresh herbs if using.
3. **Make the Dressing:**
   - In a small bowl, whisk together soy sauce, rice vinegar, sesame oil, honey or maple syrup, grated ginger, minced garlic, toasted sesame seeds, and chili flakes (if using). Adjust the seasoning to taste.
4. **Assemble the Salad:**
   - In a large salad bowl, combine the mixed salad greens, shredded carrots, cucumber, cherry tomatoes, radishes, bell pepper, and yuba.

- Drizzle the dressing over the salad and toss gently to coat all ingredients evenly.
5. **Serve:**
    - Garnish with additional toasted sesame seeds or chopped fresh cilantro/parsley if desired.
    - Serve immediately for the freshest taste.

Notes:

- **Fresh vs. Dried Yuba:** Fresh yuba can often be found in Asian markets or specialty stores. It has a more delicate texture compared to dried yuba, which requires soaking and rehydrating.
- **Customizations:** Feel free to add other vegetables or proteins such as grilled chicken, tofu cubes, or edamame for a more substantial meal.
- **Dressing Variations:** Adjust the sweetness or acidity of the dressing according to your taste. You can substitute honey with agave syrup or omit it for a less sweet dressing.
- **Storage:** If preparing in advance, keep the salad and dressing separate until ready to serve to prevent the salad from becoming soggy.

Yuba Salad is a light yet flavorful dish that showcases the unique texture of tofu skin while complementing a variety of fresh vegetables. Enjoy this refreshing and healthy salad as a side or a light main course!

Tonkotsu Ramen

Ingredients:

For the Broth:

- 4 lbs pork bones (neck bones or femur bones are ideal)
- 1 onion, halved
- 1 head of garlic, halved
- 1 thumb-sized piece of ginger, sliced
- 2-3 scallions (green onions)
- 2 tablespoons soy sauce
- 2 tablespoons mirin
- 1 tablespoon sake

For the Tare (Seasoning Sauce):

- 1/4 cup soy sauce
- 2 tablespoons miso paste (white or red)
- 1 tablespoon sake
- 1 tablespoon mirin

For the Toppings:

- 4 servings of fresh ramen noodles (or instant ramen noodles if fresh is not available)
- 4-6 slices of chashu pork (braised pork belly)
- 4 soft-boiled eggs (marinated in soy sauce, optional)
- 1 cup bamboo shoots (menma), sliced
- 1/2 cup sliced scallions (green onions)
- 1/2 cup corn kernels (optional)
- 1 sheet nori (seaweed), cut into strips
- Bean sprouts (optional)
- Sesame seeds (optional)
- A drizzle of sesame oil (optional)

Instructions:

1. **Prepare the Broth:**
   - **Blanch the Bones:** Place the pork bones in a large pot and cover with cold water. Bring to a boil, then drain and rinse the bones to remove impurities.
   - **Simmer the Broth:** Return the cleaned bones to the pot and cover with fresh cold water. Bring to a boil, then reduce to a simmer.

- **Add Aromatics:** Add onion, garlic, ginger, and scallions to the pot. Simmer on low heat for 4-6 hours, adding more water as needed to keep the bones covered. Skim off any scum that rises to the surface.
- **Strain the Broth:** After simmering, strain the broth through a fine-mesh sieve into a clean pot. Discard the solids. The broth should be creamy and opaque.

2. **Prepare the Tare:**
   - In a small bowl, combine soy sauce, miso paste, sake, and mirin. Stir until the miso paste is fully dissolved and the mixture is well combined.
3. **Prepare the Noodles and Toppings:**
   - **Cook the Noodles:** Cook the ramen noodles according to package instructions. Drain and set aside.
   - **Prepare the Toppings:** If using chashu pork, slice it into thin pieces. If you're using soft-boiled eggs, marinate them in soy sauce for at least 30 minutes. Prepare any additional toppings like bamboo shoots, corn, or bean sprouts.
4. **Assemble the Ramen:**
   - **Season the Broth:** Add the tare to the hot broth and stir to combine.
   - **Serve:** Divide the cooked ramen noodles among serving bowls. Ladle the hot broth over the noodles.
   - **Add Toppings:** Top each bowl with slices of chashu pork, soft-boiled eggs, bamboo shoots, scallions, corn, nori, and any other desired toppings.
   - **Garnish:** Drizzle with a little sesame oil and sprinkle with sesame seeds if desired.
5. **Enjoy:**
   - Serve immediately and enjoy your rich and comforting Tonkotsu Ramen!

Notes:

- **Chashu Pork:** Chashu is a traditional Japanese braised pork belly used in ramen. If you don't have chashu, you can substitute with other cooked pork or even chicken.
- **Broth Consistency:** For a richer broth, you can continue simmering the bones for longer, and you can blend the broth with an immersion blender for a smoother texture.
- **Noodles:** Fresh ramen noodles are preferred for the best texture. If using instant noodles, cook them separately and add them to the bowl just before serving to prevent them from becoming too soft.
- **Marinated Eggs:** To make marinated eggs, boil eggs for 6-7 minutes, then peel and marinate in a mixture of soy sauce, mirin, and water for at least 30 minutes.

Tonkotsu Ramen is a deeply satisfying dish that brings the rich flavors of Japan right to your kitchen. Enjoy the creamy broth, tender pork, and flavorful toppings in this classic ramen bowl!

Ebi Fry (Fried Shrimp)

Ingredients:

For the Shrimp:

- 12 large shrimp (peeled and deveined, tails left on)
- Salt and pepper, to taste
- 1/2 cup all-purpose flour
- 2 large eggs, beaten
- 1 cup panko breadcrumbs (Japanese breadcrumbs)
- Vegetable oil, for frying

For the Tonkatsu Sauce (optional):

- 1/4 cup ketchup
- 2 tablespoons Worcestershire sauce
- 1 tablespoon soy sauce
- 1 tablespoon mirin
- 1 teaspoon sugar

For Serving:

- Lemon wedges
- Shredded cabbage (optional, for garnish)

Instructions:

1. **Prepare the Shrimp:**
    - **Devein and Prep:** Peel and devein the shrimp, leaving the tails on. Lightly score the underside of each shrimp to prevent curling during frying. Pat the shrimp dry with paper towels.
    - **Season:** Season the shrimp with salt and pepper.
2. **Bread the Shrimp:**
    - Set up a breading station with three shallow dishes:
        - Place flour in the first dish.
        - Place beaten eggs in the second dish.
        - Place panko breadcrumbs in the third dish.
    - Dredge each shrimp in flour, shaking off the excess. Dip in beaten eggs, allowing excess to drip off, then coat with panko breadcrumbs, pressing gently to adhere.
3. **Heat the Oil:**
    - Heat about 1-2 inches of vegetable oil in a large, deep skillet or pot over medium-high heat. The oil should reach around 350°F (175°C). Use a thermometer to check the temperature if you have one.

4. **Fry the Shrimp:**
   - Working in batches to avoid overcrowding, carefully lower the breaded shrimp into the hot oil. Fry until golden brown and crispy, about 2-3 minutes per side. Adjust the heat as needed to maintain a consistent temperature.
   - Remove the shrimp with a slotted spoon and drain on a plate lined with paper towels.
5. **Prepare the Tonkatsu Sauce (Optional):**
   - In a small bowl, mix together ketchup, Worcestershire sauce, soy sauce, mirin, and sugar until well combined. Adjust seasoning to taste if needed.
6. **Serve:**
   - Arrange the fried shrimp on a serving plate. Serve with lemon wedges and a side of shredded cabbage if desired.
   - Provide the tonkatsu sauce for dipping, or simply squeeze fresh lemon juice over the shrimp.

Notes:

- **Shrimp Size:** Large shrimp work best for this recipe. Adjust cooking time if using smaller or larger shrimp.
- **Oil Temperature:** Maintain the oil temperature to ensure a crispy coating. If the oil is too hot, the coating may burn before the shrimp are cooked through. If too cool, the shrimp may become greasy.
- **Tonkatsu Sauce:** This sauce is optional but adds a nice tangy flavor. You can also use store-bought tonkatsu sauce or simply serve with a squeeze of lemon if you prefer.
- **Serving Ideas:** Ebi Fry is great as a main dish or appetizer. It pairs well with steamed rice, a fresh salad, or even as a filling for sandwiches.

Enjoy the crispy and delicious Ebi Fry, perfect for a satisfying meal or special occasion!

Soba Noodles with Dipping Sauce

Ingredients:

For the Soba Noodles:

- 8 oz (225 g) soba noodles
- Water for boiling

For the Dipping Sauce (Tsuyu):

- 1/2 cup soy sauce
- 1/4 cup mirin
- 1/4 cup dashi stock (or water if you prefer a milder flavor)
- 1 tablespoon sugar
- 1 teaspoon grated ginger (optional)
- 1 teaspoon toasted sesame seeds (optional)

For Garnishing (Optional):

- Thinly sliced scallions (green onions)
- Wasabi (for a bit of heat)
- Pickled ginger
- Shredded nori (seaweed)
- Sesame seeds

Instructions:

1. **Cook the Soba Noodles:**
   - Bring a large pot of water to a boil. Add the soba noodles and cook according to the package instructions, usually about 4-6 minutes, until tender but still firm.
   - Drain the noodles and rinse them under cold running water to stop the cooking process and remove excess starch. This will also help them become nice and chilled.
   - Drain thoroughly and set aside.
2. **Prepare the Dipping Sauce (Tsuyu):**
   - In a small saucepan, combine soy sauce, mirin, dashi stock (or water), and sugar.
   - Bring to a gentle boil over medium heat, stirring occasionally, until the sugar is dissolved. If using, add grated ginger at this stage.
   - Remove from heat and let the sauce cool to room temperature. If you prefer, you can refrigerate it to serve cold.
3. **Assemble and Serve:**
   - Divide the cooked soba noodles into individual serving bowls or plates.

- Serve with a small bowl of dipping sauce on the side. You can garnish the sauce with toasted sesame seeds if desired.
- Provide garnishes such as sliced scallions, wasabi, pickled ginger, shredded nori, and sesame seeds for adding to the dipping sauce as desired.
4. **Enjoy:**
    - To eat, dip a few noodles into the dipping sauce, then enjoy the combination of the savory sauce and the delicate flavor of the soba noodles.

Notes:

- **Dashi:** For a more authentic flavor, use dashi stock, which is a traditional Japanese stock made from kombu (kelp) and bonito flakes. You can find dashi powder or premade dashi in Asian markets for convenience.
- **Garnishes:** Feel free to adjust the garnishes to your taste. Fresh vegetables like cucumber or radishes can also be served alongside for added crunch and freshness.
- **Temperature:** Soba noodles are traditionally served cold with dipping sauce, but you can also serve them warm if you prefer.
- **Storage:** If you have leftovers, store the noodles and dipping sauce separately. The noodles can be kept in the refrigerator for a few days, and the sauce can be refrigerated for up to a week.

Soba Noodles with Dipping Sauce is a versatile and refreshing dish that's easy to prepare and perfect for a quick meal. Enjoy the balance of flavors and textures with this classic Japanese dish!

Nabe (Hot Pot)

Ingredients:

For the Broth:

- 4 cups dashi stock (you can use homemade or instant dashi powder mixed with water)
- 1/4 cup soy sauce
- 1/4 cup mirin
- 2 tablespoons sake
- 1 tablespoon sugar
- Salt, to taste

For the Hot Pot Ingredients:

- 1/2 pound thinly sliced beef or chicken (such as ribeye, sirloin, or chicken thighs)
- 1 cup sliced mushrooms (shiitake, enoki, or oyster mushrooms work well)
- 1 cup sliced napa cabbage
- 1 cup bok choy or spinach
- 1 cup sliced carrots
- 1 cup tofu, cut into cubes
- 1 cup sliced scallions (green onions)
- 1 cup udon noodles or rice (optional, for serving)

For Dipping Sauces (Optional):

- Ponzu sauce (citrusy soy sauce)
- Goma dare (sesame dipping sauce)
- Chopped scallions
- Grated daikon radish

Instructions:

1. **Prepare the Broth:**
   - In a large pot, combine dashi stock, soy sauce, mirin, sake, and sugar. Bring to a gentle simmer over medium heat.
   - Taste the broth and adjust seasoning with salt or additional soy sauce if needed.
2. **Prepare the Hot Pot Ingredients:**
   - Slice the beef or chicken into thin pieces if not pre-sliced.
   - Clean and slice the mushrooms.
   - Cut the vegetables into bite-sized pieces.
   - Cube the tofu.
   - Prepare any additional items like udon noodles or rice if using.
3. **Serve the Hot Pot:**

- Arrange the prepared ingredients on a large platter or separate bowls for easy access.
- Place the pot of simmering broth on a portable burner or a hot plate at the table to keep it warm.
- Allow guests to cook their own ingredients in the pot. Add items to the broth in batches, cooking until they reach the desired doneness.

4. **Dipping Sauces (Optional):**
   - Provide a selection of dipping sauces for extra flavor. Ponzu sauce and goma dare are popular choices. You can also offer chopped scallions and grated daikon radish for added texture and taste.
5. **Enjoy:**
   - Serve the cooked ingredients with a ladle of broth over bowls of rice or with udon noodles if desired. Enjoy the communal experience of cooking and eating together.

Notes:

- **Broth Variations:** You can make variations of the broth using different bases such as miso or soy milk for a different flavor profile. For a more traditional flavor, consider using kombu dashi or a chicken stock.
- **Ingredient Choices:** Feel free to customize the hot pot ingredients based on personal preference or seasonal availability. Common additions include daikon radish, sweet potato, and various types of mushrooms.
- **Safety:** Ensure that raw meat is cooked thoroughly before eating. Using separate utensils for raw and cooked ingredients helps prevent cross-contamination.
- **Leftovers:** Store leftover broth and ingredients separately. The broth can be kept in the refrigerator for a few days, and the cooked ingredients can be reheated as desired.

Nabe is not only a delicious meal but also a wonderful social experience, bringing people together around the table. Enjoy this comforting and interactive dish with family and friends!

Hiyayakko (Cold Tofu)

Ingredients:

For the Tofu:

- 1 block of firm or silken tofu (about 14 oz or 400 g)
- 1 tablespoon soy sauce
- 1 tablespoon mirin (optional, for a touch of sweetness)
- 1 teaspoon sesame oil (optional, for extra flavor)

For Toppings:

- 2 tablespoons finely chopped scallions (green onions)
- 1 tablespoon grated ginger
- 1 tablespoon bonito flakes (katsuobushi)
- 1 tablespoon shredded nori (seaweed)
- 1 teaspoon sesame seeds (optional)
- 1 tablespoon daikon radish, grated (optional)
- Pickled ginger or umeboshi (pickled plum) for garnish (optional)

Instructions:

1. **Prepare the Tofu:**
   - **Drain the Tofu:** Remove the tofu from its packaging and drain any excess water. For best results, place the tofu on a plate lined with paper towels to absorb any additional moisture.
   - **Chill:** Refrigerate the tofu for at least 30 minutes to ensure it's thoroughly chilled.
2. **Prepare the Toppings:**
   - **Chop and Grate:** Finely chop the scallions, grate the ginger, and shred the nori if not using pre-shredded. If using daikon radish, grate it and squeeze out excess moisture.
   - **Toast Sesame Seeds:** If using sesame seeds, you can toast them in a dry skillet over medium heat for a few minutes until golden and fragrant.
3. **Assemble the Dish:**
   - **Cut the Tofu:** Carefully cut the chilled tofu into cubes or slices, depending on your preference.
   - **Plate the Tofu:** Arrange the tofu on a serving plate.
4. **Add Toppings:**
   - **Top with Toppings:** Sprinkle the chopped scallions, grated ginger, bonito flakes, shredded nori, and toasted sesame seeds over the tofu. Add grated daikon radish if using.

- **Drizzle Sauce:** If desired, mix the soy sauce with mirin and sesame oil, then drizzle a small amount over the tofu. You can also serve the soy sauce mixture on the side for dipping.
5. **Serve:**
    - Serve immediately as a refreshing appetizer or side dish.

Notes:

- **Tofu Type:** Silken tofu is often used for its delicate texture, but firm tofu can be used if you prefer a denser texture. Silken tofu is more delicate and can break apart easily, so handle it gently.
- **Garnish Variations:** Feel free to customize the toppings based on your preferences or what you have on hand. Other popular toppings include minced garlic, chopped herbs, or a drizzle of ponzu sauce.
- **Soy Sauce Mixture:** Adjust the ratio of soy sauce, mirin, and sesame oil according to taste. For a less sweet option, you can omit the mirin.
- **Serving Suggestions:** Hiyayakko can be enjoyed on its own or as part of a larger meal. It pairs well with rice and other Japanese dishes.

Hiyayakko is a versatile and light dish that highlights the delicate flavor of tofu. Its simplicity allows the natural taste of the tofu to shine, enhanced by fresh and flavorful toppings. Enjoy this cool and refreshing dish as a perfect complement to any meal!

Ebi Chili

Ingredients:

For the Shrimp:

- 1 lb (450 g) large shrimp, peeled and deveined
- 1 tablespoon cornstarch
- 1 tablespoon vegetable oil

For the Chili Sauce:

- 2 tablespoons vegetable oil
- 3 cloves garlic, minced
- 1 tablespoon ginger, minced
- 2 tablespoons chili paste (such as doubanjiang or Szechuan chili paste)
- 1/4 cup ketchup
- 2 tablespoons soy sauce
- 1 tablespoon rice vinegar
- 1 tablespoon sugar
- 1/2 cup chicken or vegetable broth
- 1 tablespoon cornstarch mixed with 2 tablespoons water (for thickening)
- Salt and pepper, to taste

For Garnishing (Optional):

- Sliced scallions (green onions)
- Sesame seeds
- Fresh cilantro or parsley

Instructions:

1. **Prepare the Shrimp:**
   - **Coat the Shrimp:** Toss the peeled and deveined shrimp with 1 tablespoon of cornstarch until evenly coated.
   - **Cook the Shrimp:** Heat 1 tablespoon of vegetable oil in a large skillet or wok over medium-high heat. Add the shrimp and cook until pink and opaque, about 2-3 minutes per side. Remove the shrimp from the skillet and set aside.
2. **Prepare the Chili Sauce:**
   - **Sauté Aromatics:** In the same skillet, add 2 tablespoons of vegetable oil. Heat over medium heat. Add the minced garlic and ginger, and sauté for 30 seconds until fragrant.
   - **Add Chili Paste:** Stir in the chili paste and cook for an additional 1-2 minutes.

- **Add Sauce Ingredients:** Add ketchup, soy sauce, rice vinegar, sugar, and chicken or vegetable broth. Stir to combine and bring the mixture to a simmer.
    - **Thicken the Sauce:** Mix the cornstarch with water to create a slurry, then add it to the sauce. Stir constantly until the sauce thickens, about 1-2 minutes.
3. **Combine Shrimp and Sauce:**
    - **Return Shrimp to Skillet:** Add the cooked shrimp back into the skillet with the sauce. Stir to coat the shrimp evenly with the sauce. Simmer for 1-2 minutes to heat through and allow the flavors to meld.
4. **Season and Garnish:**
    - **Adjust Seasoning:** Taste the sauce and adjust seasoning with salt and pepper as needed.
    - **Garnish:** Garnish with sliced scallions, sesame seeds, and fresh cilantro or parsley if desired.
5. **Serve:**
    - Serve hot with steamed rice or noodles.

Notes:

- **Chili Paste:** Adjust the amount of chili paste to suit your spice preference. Doubanjiang is a popular choice for its rich, umami flavor, but you can use other types of chili paste or sauce if preferred.
- **Thickening:** If you prefer a thicker sauce, you can add a bit more cornstarch slurry. If it becomes too thick, thin it out with a bit more broth.
- **Vegetarian Option:** To make a vegetarian version, you can substitute the shrimp with tofu or vegetables and adjust the cooking time accordingly.
- **Serving Suggestions:** Ebi Chili pairs well with simple sides like steamed rice, white or brown rice, or even noodles.

Ebi Chili is a flavorful and satisfying dish that offers a delightful balance of heat, sweetness, and tanginess. Enjoy this spicy shrimp dish as part of a delicious meal!

Miso Glazed Black Cod

Ingredients:

For the Miso Marinade:

- 1/2 cup white miso paste
- 1/4 cup sake
- 1/4 cup mirin
- 3 tablespoons sugar

For the Black Cod:

- 4 black cod fillets (about 6 oz each)
- 1 tablespoon vegetable oil (for brushing)

Garnish (Optional):

- Sliced scallions (green onions)
- Sesame seeds
- Lemon wedges

Instructions:

1. **Prepare the Miso Marinade:**
   - In a small saucepan, combine the white miso paste, sake, mirin, and sugar.
   - Heat over medium heat, stirring constantly until the sugar is dissolved and the mixture is smooth and slightly thickened. Remove from heat and let it cool to room temperature.
2. **Marinate the Black Cod:**
   - Pat the black cod fillets dry with paper towels.
   - Place the fillets in a resealable plastic bag or shallow dish and pour the cooled miso marinade over them.
   - Seal the bag or cover the dish and refrigerate. Marinate the cod for at least 2 hours, preferably overnight for the best flavor.
3. **Prepare for Broiling:**
   - Preheat your broiler to high heat. Line a baking sheet with aluminum foil and place a wire rack on top of the baking sheet. This helps catch any drips and allows for even cooking.
   - Remove the black cod fillets from the marinade and gently wipe off excess marinade. Brush the fillets with a light coating of vegetable oil to help with browning.
4. **Broil the Black Cod:**
   - Place the marinated black cod fillets on the wire rack.

- Broil the fish for 5-7 minutes, or until the top is caramelized and the fish is cooked through. The internal temperature should reach about 145°F (63°C). The fish should flake easily with a fork.

5. **Garnish and Serve:**
   - Transfer the broiled black cod to serving plates.
   - Garnish with sliced scallions, sesame seeds, and lemon wedges if desired.
   - Serve with steamed rice and your favorite vegetables or salad.

Notes:

- **Miso Type:** White miso paste is preferred for its mild flavor and sweetness, but you can use yellow miso paste if you like a slightly stronger flavor.
- **Marinating Time:** For the best results, marinate the fish overnight. However, if you're short on time, a minimum of 2 hours will still provide good flavor.
- **Broiling Tips:** Keep an eye on the fish while broiling to prevent burning. If the fillets are browning too quickly, you can move them to a lower rack or reduce the broiler temperature slightly.
- **Alternative Cooking Method:** If you prefer not to broil, you can also bake the marinated fish in a preheated oven at 400°F (200°C) for 12-15 minutes, or until cooked through.

Miso Glazed Black Cod is a flavorful and sophisticated dish that highlights the delicate taste of black cod with a rich miso glaze. Enjoy this exquisite dish with simple sides to let the flavors shine!

Japanese Style Fried Rice

Ingredients:

For the Fried Rice:

- 2 cups cooked rice (preferably cold or day-old rice works best)
- 2 tablespoons vegetable oil
- 1/2 cup diced onion
- 1/2 cup diced carrot
- 1/2 cup diced bell pepper (any color)
- 1/2 cup frozen peas
- 2 cloves garlic, minced
- 1/2 cup cooked chicken, pork, shrimp, or tofu (diced)
- 2 large eggs
- 2-3 green onions (scallions), sliced
- 1 tablespoon soy sauce
- 1 tablespoon oyster sauce (optional)
- 1 teaspoon sesame oil
- Salt and pepper, to taste

For Garnishing (Optional):

- Additional sliced green onions
- Sesame seeds
- Pickled ginger

Instructions:

1. **Prepare the Ingredients:**
   - If using leftover rice, break up any clumps so that the grains are separated. Cold or day-old rice is ideal for frying because it is less likely to become mushy.
   - Dice the vegetables and cook any meat or tofu you are using, if not already cooked.
2. **Cook the Vegetables and Meat:**
   - Heat 2 tablespoons of vegetable oil in a large skillet or wok over medium-high heat.
   - Add the diced onion and cook until it becomes translucent, about 2-3 minutes.
   - Add the diced carrot, bell pepper, and frozen peas. Stir-fry for an additional 3-4 minutes until the vegetables are tender-crisp.
   - Add the minced garlic and cook for another 30 seconds until fragrant.
   - Add the cooked meat or tofu and stir to combine.
3. **Scramble the Eggs:**
   - Push the vegetables and meat to one side of the skillet or wok.

- Add a bit more oil if needed, and crack the eggs into the empty side of the skillet.
- Scramble the eggs with a spatula and cook until just set. Then mix the eggs with the vegetables and meat.

4. **Add the Rice:**
   - Add the cold rice to the skillet or wok. Break up any remaining clumps and stir-fry to combine with the vegetables and meat.
   - Pour the soy sauce and optional oyster sauce over the rice. Stir well to evenly distribute the sauces and flavor the rice.

5. **Finish with Seasonings:**
   - Drizzle the sesame oil over the fried rice and stir to combine.
   - Taste and season with salt and pepper as needed.

6. **Garnish and Serve:**
   - Transfer the fried rice to serving plates or bowls.
   - Garnish with additional sliced green onions, sesame seeds, and pickled ginger if desired.

Notes:

- **Rice Texture:** Using cold, day-old rice helps prevent the fried rice from becoming mushy. If you use freshly cooked rice, spread it out on a tray to cool and dry slightly before using.
- **Meat/Tofu:** Customize the fried rice by using your favorite protein. Pre-cooked meats or tofu are ideal, but you can cook raw meat or tofu in the skillet before adding the rice.
- **Vegetables:** Feel free to use other vegetables like mushrooms, corn, or bean sprouts based on what you have on hand.
- **Sauces:** Adjust the amount of soy sauce and oyster sauce to your taste. If you prefer a vegetarian version, omit the oyster sauce or use a vegetarian substitute.

Japanese-style fried rice is a quick and satisfying meal that can be easily customized to suit your preferences. Enjoy this versatile dish as a tasty main course or a delicious side!

Gyudon (Beef Bowl)

Ingredients:

For the Beef Bowl:

- 1 lb (450 g) thinly sliced beef (such as ribeye, sirloin, or shabu-shabu beef)
- 1 large onion, thinly sliced
- 2 tablespoons vegetable oil
- 1 cup dashi stock (or beef broth)
- 1/4 cup soy sauce
- 1/4 cup mirin
- 2 tablespoons sugar
- 1 tablespoon sake (optional, for added depth of flavor)
- Cooked rice (steamed, for serving)

For Garnishing (Optional):

- Sliced green onions (scallions)
- Pickled ginger (beni shoga)
- Shredded nori (seaweed)
- A raw egg or a soft-boiled egg (for traditional topping)

Instructions:

1. **Prepare the Ingredients:**
   - Thinly slice the beef if not pre-sliced.
   - Thinly slice the onion.
   - Prepare the rice and keep it warm.
2. **Cook the Beef and Onions:**
   - Heat 2 tablespoons of vegetable oil in a large skillet or wok over medium heat.
   - Add the sliced onions and cook until they become translucent and slightly caramelized, about 5-7 minutes.
   - Add the sliced beef to the skillet. Cook until the beef is no longer pink, stirring frequently to ensure even cooking.
3. **Prepare the Sauce:**
   - In a small bowl, combine dashi stock (or beef broth), soy sauce, mirin, sugar, and sake (if using).
   - Pour the sauce mixture over the beef and onions in the skillet. Stir to combine.
4. **Simmer:**
   - Bring the mixture to a simmer and cook for 5-7 minutes, or until the beef is tender and the sauce has slightly thickened. Adjust the seasoning with additional soy sauce or sugar if needed.
5. **Serve:**

- Spoon the cooked beef and onions over bowls of steamed rice.
- Garnish with sliced green onions, pickled ginger, and shredded nori if desired.
- Top with a raw egg or a soft-boiled egg for a traditional touch, if using.

Notes:

- **Beef Type:** Use thinly sliced beef to ensure quick cooking and tenderness. Pre-sliced beef for shabu-shabu or sukiyaki works well.
- **Dashi:** Dashi stock adds authentic umami flavor, but you can use beef broth or water if dashi is not available. If using instant dashi powder, follow the package instructions to make 1 cup of dashi.
- **Egg:** A raw egg or a soft-boiled egg adds richness and a traditional touch to the dish. To soft-boil an egg, cook it in boiling water for 6-7 minutes, then cool in ice water before peeling.
- **Adjustments:** Modify the sweetness or saltiness of the sauce according to your taste by adjusting the amount of sugar or soy sauce.

Gyudon is a comforting and flavorful dish that highlights the savory and slightly sweet flavors of the beef and sauce. It's a classic Japanese comfort food that's quick to make and always satisfying. Enjoy this delicious beef bowl with your favorite garnishes and sides!

Chicken Teriyaki

Ingredients:

For the Teriyaki Sauce:

- 1/4 cup soy sauce
- 1/4 cup mirin (sweet rice wine)
- 2 tablespoons sake (optional, for additional depth)
- 2 tablespoons sugar (or honey)
- 1 teaspoon cornstarch mixed with 1 tablespoon water (for thickening, optional)

For the Chicken:

- 4 boneless, skinless chicken thighs or breasts
- 1 tablespoon vegetable oil (for cooking)
- Salt and pepper, to taste
- Sesame seeds (for garnish, optional)
- Sliced green onions (for garnish, optional)

For Serving:

- Cooked rice
- Steamed or stir-fried vegetables (such as broccoli, bell peppers, or carrots)

Instructions:

1. **Prepare the Teriyaki Sauce:**
   - In a small saucepan, combine soy sauce, mirin, sake (if using), and sugar.
   - Bring the mixture to a simmer over medium heat, stirring until the sugar is dissolved.
   - If you prefer a thicker sauce, mix cornstarch with water to create a slurry and add it to the sauce. Stir until the sauce thickens slightly. Remove from heat and let it cool.
2. **Prepare the Chicken:**
   - Pat the chicken dry with paper towels. Season both sides with a little salt and pepper.
   - If using chicken breasts, you can pound them to an even thickness for more uniform cooking.
3. **Cook the Chicken:**
   - Heat vegetable oil in a large skillet or grill pan over medium-high heat.
   - Add the chicken and cook for about 5-7 minutes on each side, or until the chicken is cooked through and has a nice golden brown color. Chicken should reach an internal temperature of 165°F (74°C).

- While the chicken is cooking, you can occasionally brush it with some of the teriyaki sauce for added flavor.
4. **Glaze the Chicken:**
    - Once the chicken is cooked through, remove it from the skillet and let it rest for a few minutes.
    - Brush or drizzle the cooked chicken with the remaining teriyaki sauce. You can also return the chicken to the skillet and cook for an additional minute or so to allow the sauce to caramelize slightly.
5. **Serve:**
    - Slice the chicken into strips and place it on a serving plate.
    - Garnish with sesame seeds and sliced green onions if desired.
    - Serve the chicken teriyaki with cooked rice and your favorite vegetables.

Notes:

- **Chicken Cut:** Chicken thighs are typically used for their juiciness and flavor, but chicken breasts work well too if you prefer a leaner option.
- **Mirin Substitute:** If you don't have mirin, you can substitute with a combination of white wine and a small amount of sugar, or just use extra sugar.
- **Sauce Variations:** Adjust the sweetness and saltiness of the teriyaki sauce according to your taste. You can also add a splash of rice vinegar for a hint of tanginess.
- **Serving Suggestions:** Chicken teriyaki pairs well with steamed white rice, brown rice, or even noodles. Add a side of stir-fried or steamed vegetables for a complete meal.

Chicken Teriyaki is a flavorful and satisfying dish that's easy to make at home. The sweet and savory glaze makes the chicken irresistible, and it's a great way to enjoy a taste of Japanese cuisine.

Spicy Tuna Don

Ingredients:

For the Spicy Tuna:

- 1/2 lb (225 g) sushi-grade tuna, diced into small cubes
- 2 tablespoons mayonnaise
- 1 tablespoon sriracha (adjust to taste for spiciness)
- 1 teaspoon soy sauce
- 1 teaspoon sesame oil
- 1 teaspoon rice vinegar
- 1 teaspoon sesame seeds (optional)
- 1 tablespoon chopped green onions (optional)
- 1 teaspoon chopped fresh cilantro or parsley (optional)

For Serving:

- 2 cups cooked rice (steamed, for serving)
- Sliced cucumber
- Shredded carrots
- Sliced avocado
- Pickled ginger (optional)
- Nori (seaweed) strips or sheets, cut into thin strips (optional)
- Soy sauce for drizzling

Instructions:

1. **Prepare the Spicy Tuna:**
   - In a bowl, combine the mayonnaise, sriracha, soy sauce, sesame oil, and rice vinegar.
   - Gently fold in the diced tuna, ensuring each piece is well coated with the spicy mayo mixture.
   - If desired, mix in sesame seeds, chopped green onions, and fresh cilantro or parsley for added flavor and texture.
   - Cover the bowl and refrigerate the spicy tuna mixture while you prepare the rest of the dish.
2. **Prepare the Rice and Toppings:**
   - If not already done, cook the rice according to package instructions and keep it warm.
   - Prepare your choice of toppings such as sliced cucumber, shredded carrots, and sliced avocado.
3. **Assemble the Spicy Tuna Don:**
   - Divide the cooked rice between serving bowls.

- Spoon the spicy tuna mixture over the rice.
- Arrange the sliced cucumber, shredded carrots, and avocado around the tuna on each bowl.
4. **Garnish and Serve:**
    - Garnish with pickled ginger, nori strips, and additional sesame seeds if desired.
    - Drizzle a little soy sauce over the top for extra flavor.
    - Serve immediately and enjoy!

Notes:

- **Sushi-Grade Tuna:** Ensure you use sushi-grade tuna or fresh tuna that is safe for raw consumption. The quality of the tuna greatly impacts the overall flavor of the dish.
- **Spice Level:** Adjust the amount of sriracha based on your preferred level of spiciness. You can also add a bit of chopped fresh chili or chili oil for extra heat.
- **Rice Type:** Short-grain or medium-grain Japanese rice is preferred for its stickiness, but you can use other types of rice if necessary.
- **Toppings:** Feel free to customize the toppings according to your preference. Other popular options include edamame, radish slices, or seaweed salad.

Spicy Tuna Don is a delicious and versatile dish that offers a delightful mix of flavors and textures. The creamy, spicy tuna paired with fresh vegetables and warm rice makes for a satisfying meal that's both flavorful and easy to prepare.

Zaru Soba (Chilled Soba Noodles)

Ingredients:

For the Soba Noodles:

- 8 oz (225 g) soba noodles (buckwheat noodles)
- 4 cups water (for boiling)

For the Tsuyu (Dipping Sauce):

- 1/4 cup soy sauce
- 1/4 cup mirin
- 1/4 cup dashi stock (or water for a lighter version)
- 1 tablespoon sugar (optional, for added sweetness)

For Garnishing and Serving:

- Sliced green onions
- Grated daikon radish
- Wasabi
- Nori (seaweed) strips
- Pickled ginger (optional)

Instructions:

1. **Prepare the Soba Noodles:**
    - Bring a large pot of water to a boil.
    - Add the soba noodles to the boiling water and cook according to the package instructions, usually 4-5 minutes. Stir occasionally to prevent sticking.
    - Test the noodles for doneness; they should be tender but still have a slight bite (al dente).
    - Drain the noodles in a colander and rinse them thoroughly under cold running water to stop the cooking process and cool them down. Rinse until the water runs clear to remove excess starch.
2. **Prepare the Tsuyu (Dipping Sauce):**
    - In a small saucepan, combine soy sauce, mirin, and dashi stock. If using sugar, add it to the mixture.
    - Heat the mixture over medium heat, stirring occasionally, until it begins to simmer. Allow it to cool completely before serving.
    - You can also prepare the tsuyu ahead of time and refrigerate it until ready to use.
3. **Prepare the Garnishes:**
    - Slice the green onions thinly.
    - Grate the daikon radish.

        - Cut the nori seaweed into thin strips.
4. **Assemble and Serve:**
    - Arrange the chilled soba noodles on a serving plate or bamboo mat (zaru) if available.
    - Serve the tsuyu dipping sauce in small bowls.
    - Place the garnishes (green onions, grated daikon, wasabi, and nori strips) in small dishes alongside the noodles.
    - To eat, dip a few noodles into the tsuyu sauce and enjoy with the garnishes.

Notes:

- **Soba Noodles:** Soba noodles are available at most Asian grocery stores. They can be either 100% buckwheat or a blend of buckwheat and wheat flour. Check the package for specific cooking instructions.
- **Tsuyu Variations:** You can adjust the sweetness and saltiness of the tsuyu by varying the amount of sugar and soy sauce. If you prefer a stronger flavor, you can use more dashi or soy sauce.
- **Garnishes:** Customize the garnishes according to your taste. Additional options include thinly sliced shiso leaves or a sprinkle of sesame seeds.
- **Serving:** Zaru Soba is typically served cold on a bamboo mat (zaru) or a plate, and the dipping sauce is served separately in individual bowls.

Zaru Soba is a simple yet flavorful dish that highlights the delicate taste of soba noodles and the savory umami of the dipping sauce. It's a refreshing choice for a light meal or as part of a larger Japanese meal. Enjoy the contrast of the cool noodles with the savory dipping sauce and fresh garnishes!

Shabu-Shabu Salad

Ingredients:

For the Shabu-Shabu Beef:

- 8 oz (225 g) thinly sliced beef (such as ribeye, sirloin, or shabu-shabu beef)
- 4 cups water (for blanching)
- 1 tablespoon soy sauce
- 1 tablespoon mirin
- 1 teaspoon sesame oil

For the Salad:

- 2 cups mixed salad greens (such as romaine, arugula, and spinach)
- 1 cup shredded cabbage
- 1/2 cup thinly sliced carrots
- 1/2 cup sliced cucumber
- 1/2 cup cherry tomatoes, halved
- 1/4 cup thinly sliced red onion
- 1/4 cup sliced radishes (optional)
- 2 tablespoons sesame seeds (for garnish)
- 2 tablespoons chopped fresh cilantro (optional, for garnish)

For the Dressing:

- 3 tablespoons rice vinegar
- 2 tablespoons soy sauce
- 1 tablespoon sesame oil
- 1 tablespoon honey or sugar
- 1 teaspoon grated fresh ginger
- 1 clove garlic, minced
- 1 teaspoon toasted sesame seeds (optional)

Instructions:

1. **Prepare the Shabu-Shabu Beef:**
    - Bring 4 cups of water to a boil in a medium saucepan.
    - Add the beef slices to the boiling water, cooking for about 30 seconds to 1 minute, or until just cooked through. The beef should be tender but not overcooked.
    - Remove the beef slices from the water using a slotted spoon and transfer them to a bowl of ice water to cool and stop the cooking process. Drain and pat dry with paper towels.

- In a small bowl, combine the soy sauce, mirin, and sesame oil. Toss the cooked beef slices in the sauce mixture to coat.
2. **Prepare the Dressing:**
    - In a small bowl, whisk together rice vinegar, soy sauce, sesame oil, honey or sugar, grated ginger, and minced garlic.
    - Taste and adjust seasoning as needed. For extra flavor, you can add toasted sesame seeds.
3. **Prepare the Salad:**
    - In a large salad bowl, combine the mixed salad greens, shredded cabbage, sliced carrots, cucumber, cherry tomatoes, red onion, and radishes if using.
    - Toss the vegetables lightly to mix.
4. **Assemble the Salad:**
    - Arrange the salad vegetables on individual serving plates or leave them in the salad bowl.
    - Top with the chilled, sauced shabu-shabu beef slices.
    - Drizzle the dressing over the salad or serve it on the side.
5. **Garnish and Serve:**
    - Garnish with sesame seeds and chopped cilantro if desired.
    - Serve immediately, or chill the salad in the refrigerator until ready to serve.

Notes:

- **Beef:** Thinly sliced beef is essential for the quick cooking technique. If you don't have access to shabu-shabu beef, you can use other thinly sliced cuts of beef.
- **Vegetables:** Feel free to customize the salad with additional vegetables like bell peppers, snap peas, or avocado based on your preference.
- **Dressing:** Adjust the sweetness and tanginess of the dressing to your taste. You can also add a touch of soy sauce or extra honey for flavor balance.
- **Make-Ahead:** You can prepare the beef and dressing in advance and keep them in the refrigerator. Assemble the salad just before serving to maintain the freshness of the vegetables.

Shabu-Shabu Salad is a light and refreshing dish that combines the savory flavors of cooked beef with crisp, fresh vegetables and a zesty dressing. It's perfect as a main course for a light lunch or as a side dish for dinner. Enjoy this flavorful and nutritious salad!

Japanese Cheesecake

Ingredients:

For the Cheesecake:

- 8 oz (225 g) cream cheese, softened
- 1/2 cup (120 ml) milk
- 1/4 cup (50 g) granulated sugar
- 1/4 cup (30 g) all-purpose flour
- 3 large eggs, separated
- 1/4 teaspoon cream of tartar (optional, for stabilizing egg whites)
- 1/4 cup (50 g) granulated sugar (for egg whites)

For the Water Bath:

- Boiling water (for the water bath)

Optional for Garnish:

- Powdered sugar (for dusting)
- Fresh berries or fruit

Instructions:

1. **Prepare the Oven and Pans:**
   - Preheat your oven to 320°F (160°C).
   - Grease the sides of a 9-inch (23 cm) round cake pan and line the bottom with parchment paper. For a smoother finish, you can wrap the outside of the pan with aluminum foil to prevent water from seeping in during the water bath.
2. **Prepare the Cheesecake Batter:**
   - In a medium saucepan, heat the milk over low heat until warm (not boiling).
   - Add the softened cream cheese and stir until completely melted and smooth. Remove from heat and let it cool slightly.
   - In a separate bowl, sift together the flour and 1/4 cup (50 g) sugar. Gradually add this mixture to the cream cheese mixture, stirring until well combined.
   - Whisk the egg yolks and add them to the cream cheese mixture, mixing until smooth.
3. **Whip the Egg Whites:**
   - In a clean mixing bowl, beat the egg whites with an electric mixer on medium speed until frothy.
   - If using cream of tartar, add it at this stage to stabilize the egg whites.
   - Gradually add 1/4 cup (50 g) sugar and continue to beat until stiff peaks form.
4. **Fold Egg Whites into Batter:**

- Gently fold one-third of the beaten egg whites into the cream cheese mixture to lighten it.
- Carefully fold in the remaining egg whites in two additions, being cautious not to deflate the mixture too much. The batter should be light and airy.

5. **Bake the Cheesecake:**
   - Pour the batter into the prepared cake pan.
   - Place the cake pan in a larger roasting pan or baking dish. Pour hot water into the larger pan to create a water bath, ensuring it reaches halfway up the sides of the cake pan.
   - Bake in the preheated oven for 50-60 minutes, or until the cheesecake is set and lightly golden on top. The center should be slightly jiggly but not liquid.

6. **Cool and Serve:**
   - Turn off the oven and leave the cheesecake in the oven with the door slightly ajar for 1 hour to cool gradually. This helps prevent cracking.
   - Remove the cheesecake from the oven and water bath. Allow it to cool completely at room temperature, then refrigerate for at least 4 hours or overnight to set further.
   - Before serving, dust with powdered sugar and garnish with fresh berries or fruit if desired.

Notes:

- **Cream Cheese:** Ensure the cream cheese is fully softened to avoid lumps in the batter. It should be at room temperature before mixing.
- **Water Bath:** The water bath helps to create a moist environment that prevents the cheesecake from drying out and cracking. Make sure the water does not get into the cake pan.
- **Egg Whites:** Be sure the mixing bowl and beaters are completely clean and dry when whipping the egg whites to ensure they whip up properly.
- **Serving:** Japanese Cheesecake is best enjoyed chilled. It has a light, fluffy texture and a subtle, creamy flavor that pairs well with fresh fruit or a light dusting of powdered sugar.

Japanese Cheesecake is a delightful dessert that's both elegant and approachable. Its soft, airy texture and delicate flavor make it a favorite for special occasions or a sweet treat to enjoy with friends and family.

Matcha Tiramisu

Ingredients:

For the Matcha Mascarpone Mixture:

- 8 oz (225 g) mascarpone cheese, softened
- 1 cup (240 ml) heavy cream
- 1/2 cup (60 g) powdered sugar
- 2 tablespoons matcha powder (adjust to taste)

For the Coffee Mixture:

- 1 cup (240 ml) strong brewed coffee, cooled
- 2 tablespoons sugar (optional, to taste)
- 2 tablespoons coffee liqueur (optional, such as Kahlúa or Marsala wine)

For Assembly:

- 1 package (7 oz/200 g) ladyfingers (savoiardi)
- Additional matcha powder for dusting

Optional Garnishes:

- Fresh berries
- Whipped cream
- Mint leaves

Instructions:

1. **Prepare the Coffee Mixture:**
   - In a shallow dish, combine the brewed coffee, sugar (if using), and coffee liqueur (if using). Stir until the sugar is dissolved. Set aside.
2. **Prepare the Matcha Mascarpone Mixture:**
   - In a medium bowl, sift the matcha powder to remove any lumps.
   - In a separate large bowl, beat the mascarpone cheese with an electric mixer until smooth and creamy.
   - In another bowl, whip the heavy cream with an electric mixer until soft peaks form.
   - Gently fold the sifted matcha powder and powdered sugar into the mascarpone cheese until well combined.
   - Carefully fold the whipped cream into the matcha mascarpone mixture until fully incorporated. Be gentle to maintain the light and airy texture.
3. **Assemble the Tiramisu:**

- Quickly dip each ladyfinger into the coffee mixture, ensuring they are coated but not soaked (they should still be slightly firm).
- Arrange a layer of dipped ladyfingers in the bottom of a serving dish or individual serving glasses.
- Spread half of the matcha mascarpone mixture over the layer of ladyfingers.
- Repeat with another layer of dipped ladyfingers and the remaining matcha mascarpone mixture.

4. **Chill and Serve:**
    - Cover the dish with plastic wrap and refrigerate for at least 4 hours, or overnight, to allow the flavors to meld and the tiramisu to set.
    - Before serving, dust the top with additional matcha powder using a fine sieve. You can also garnish with fresh berries, whipped cream, or mint leaves if desired.

Notes:

- **Matcha Powder:** Use high-quality matcha powder for the best flavor and color. Adjust the amount of matcha to your taste preference; more matcha will give a stronger green tea flavor.
- **Ladyfingers:** If ladyfingers are not available, you can use sponge cake or cake cubes as an alternative. Just ensure they are lightly soaked in the coffee mixture.
- **Coffee:** Make sure the coffee is cooled before dipping the ladyfingers to prevent them from becoming too soggy.
- **Serving:** Matcha Tiramisu can be made in a large dish or individual serving glasses. The individual servings are great for parties or special occasions.

Matcha Tiramisu combines the creamy richness of traditional tiramisu with the unique flavor of matcha, creating a dessert that's both visually stunning and delicious. It's a wonderful way to enjoy a classic treat with a Japanese twist!

Mochi Ice Cream

Ingredients:

For the Mochi Dough:

- 1 cup (120 g) glutinous rice flour (also called sweet rice flour or mochiko)
- 1/4 cup (50 g) granulated sugar
- 1 cup (240 ml) water
- Cornstarch or potato starch (for dusting)

For the Ice Cream Filling:

- 1 pint (475 ml) ice cream (flavor of your choice, such as vanilla, matcha, chocolate, or red bean)

Instructions:

1. **Prepare the Ice Cream:**
   - Scoop out the ice cream and form it into small balls, about 1 inch (2.5 cm) in diameter.
   - Place the ice cream balls on a baking sheet lined with parchment paper and freeze until firm, at least 2 hours.
2. **Prepare the Mochi Dough:**
   - In a microwave-safe bowl, mix the glutinous rice flour and granulated sugar.
   - Gradually add the water to the mixture, stirring until smooth and well combined.
   - Cover the bowl with plastic wrap and microwave on high for 1 minute. Stir the mixture, then cover and microwave for an additional 1 minute. Stir again, then microwave for 30 seconds more, or until the mixture becomes thick and translucent.
   - Let the mochi dough cool slightly until it is manageable but still warm.
3. **Assemble the Mochi Ice Cream:**
   - Dust a clean work surface with cornstarch or potato starch to prevent sticking.
   - Turn the mochi dough out onto the dusted surface and lightly dust the top of the dough with more starch.
   - Roll out the mochi dough to about 1/4 inch (6 mm) thickness. If the dough is too sticky, dust it lightly with more starch.
   - Use a round cutter or glass (about 3 inches/7.5 cm in diameter) to cut out circles of mochi dough.
   - Place a chilled ice cream ball in the center of each mochi circle.
   - Gently stretch and fold the edges of the mochi dough around the ice cream, pinching to seal the edges. You may need to use a bit of starch to help with the handling and sealing process.
   - Place each filled mochi ice cream ball back on the parchment-lined baking sheet.

4. **Freeze and Serve:**
    - Return the assembled mochi ice cream balls to the freezer and freeze until firm, at least 1 hour, or until ready to serve.
    - When ready to serve, remove the mochi ice cream from the freezer and let it sit at room temperature for a few minutes to soften slightly for easier eating.

Notes:

- **Glutinous Rice Flour:** Use glutinous rice flour (mochiko) rather than regular rice flour. It is essential for achieving the chewy texture of the mochi dough.
- **Handling Mochi:** Mochi dough can be sticky, so keep your hands and work surface dusted with cornstarch or potato starch to prevent sticking.
- **Ice Cream Flavor:** Choose ice cream flavors that complement the mochi dough. Traditional flavors include matcha, red bean, and vanilla, but you can experiment with other flavors as well.
- **Storage:** Mochi ice cream can be stored in the freezer for up to a month. To prevent them from sticking together, you may want to place parchment paper between the mochi ice cream balls.

Mochi Ice Cream is a fun and delicious dessert that's sure to impress with its unique texture and delightful flavor combinations. Enjoy making and eating these delightful treats!

Kakigori (Shaved Ice)

Ingredients:

For the Shaved Ice:

- 1 block of ice (store-bought or homemade ice block)
- 1 cup (240 ml) water (if making flavored ice)

For the Flavored Syrups:

- **Classic Syrup:**
    - 1 cup (200 g) granulated sugar
    - 1 cup (240 ml) water
    - 1 teaspoon vanilla extract (optional)
- **Matcha Syrup:**
    - 1/2 cup (100 g) granulated sugar
    - 1/2 cup (120 ml) water
    - 1 tablespoon matcha powder
- **Strawberry Syrup:**
    - 1 cup (200 g) granulated sugar
    - 1 cup (240 ml) fresh or frozen strawberries, pureed

For Toppings:

- Sweetened condensed milk
- Red bean paste (anko)
- Fresh fruit (e.g., strawberries, mango, kiwi)
- Sweetened adzuki beans
- Jelly cubes
- Pocky sticks or other snacks

Instructions:

1. **Prepare the Ice Block:**
    - If you don't have a block of ice, you can freeze water in a large container to create your own ice block. Freeze for at least 4-6 hours or until solid.
    - To make flavored ice, mix water with a flavoring (e.g., fruit juice or syrup) and freeze in a container. This adds extra flavor to the ice itself.
2. **Make the Flavored Syrups:**
    - **Classic Syrup:** Combine granulated sugar and water in a saucepan over medium heat. Stir until the sugar is dissolved. Allow the syrup to cool, then stir in vanilla extract if desired.

- **Matcha Syrup:** Heat water and sugar in a saucepan until the sugar dissolves. Whisk in matcha powder until smooth. Allow the syrup to cool.
- **Strawberry Syrup:** Blend strawberries until smooth. Combine with sugar in a saucepan and heat gently until the sugar dissolves. Allow to cool.

3. **Shave the Ice:**
   - Use a shaved ice machine to shave the ice into a fluffy, snow-like texture. If you don't have a shaved ice machine, you can use a blender or food processor to crush the ice, but the texture may not be as fine.
4. **Assemble the Kakigori:**
   - Scoop the shaved ice into serving bowls or cups.
   - Drizzle the flavored syrups over the shaved ice. You can use one flavor or a combination of flavors.
   - Add toppings of your choice, such as sweetened condensed milk, red bean paste, fresh fruit, or jelly cubes.
5. **Serve Immediately:**
   - Kakigori is best enjoyed immediately while the ice is fluffy and the flavors are fresh.

Notes:

- **Shaved Ice Machine:** A good quality shaved ice machine will produce the light, fluffy texture that is characteristic of traditional kakigori. If using a blender, crush the ice until fine, but be aware that it may not be as airy.
- **Flavored Ice:** For extra flavor, you can freeze flavored liquids (like fruit juice) into ice blocks and then shave them. This adds an additional layer of flavor to the dessert.
- **Toppings:** Feel free to get creative with your toppings. Kakigori is versatile and can be customized with various sweet and savory toppings.
- **Storage:** If you have leftover shaved ice, it can be stored in the freezer for a short period, but it may lose its fluffy texture. It's best enjoyed fresh.

Kakigori is a refreshing and customizable dessert that's perfect for hot days or as a sweet treat. Its light, airy texture and variety of flavors make it a popular choice for cooling down and enjoying a bit of sweetness.

Red Bean Soup (Zenzai)

Ingredients:

For the Soup:

- 1 cup (200 g) adzuki beans
- 4 cups (960 ml) water (for boiling beans)
- 3 cups (720 ml) water (for simmering beans)
- 1/2 cup (100 g) granulated sugar (adjust to taste)
- 1/4 teaspoon salt (optional, to enhance flavor)

For Serving:

- Mochi (sweet rice cakes) or shiratama dango (sweet rice flour dumplings)
- Additional sweeteners (e.g., honey or maple syrup) if desired

Instructions:

1. **Prepare the Adzuki Beans:**
    - Rinse the adzuki beans under cold water. Pick out any debris or damaged beans.
    - In a large pot, cover the beans with 4 cups of water. Bring to a boil over medium-high heat. Boil for 2 minutes, then remove from heat and let the beans soak for 1 hour. This helps to reduce the cooking time and make the beans more tender.
2. **Cook the Beans:**
    - After soaking, drain and rinse the beans. Return them to the pot and add 3 cups of fresh water.
    - Bring the water to a boil over medium-high heat. Reduce the heat to low and simmer, covered, for about 1 to 1.5 hours, or until the beans are tender. Stir occasionally and add more water if needed to keep the beans submerged.
3. **Make the Soup:**
    - Once the beans are tender, use a ladle or spoon to mash some of the beans against the side of the pot. This helps thicken the soup and create a smoother texture. For a chunkier texture, mash fewer beans.
    - Stir in the granulated sugar and salt (if using). Adjust the sweetness to taste. Continue to simmer for an additional 10-15 minutes, until the soup is slightly thickened.
4. **Prepare the Mochi or Dumplings (Optional):**
    - If using mochi or shiratama dango, prepare them according to the package instructions or recipe. For mochi, you can use store-bought or make it fresh. For shiratama dango, mix the sweet rice flour with water, form into small balls, and cook them in boiling water until they float.
5. **Serve:**

- Ladle the red bean soup into bowls.
- Add mochi or dumplings on top or on the side, if desired.
- Serve hot. If serving cold, allow the soup to cool and refrigerate before serving.

Notes:

- **Beans:** Adzuki beans are small, red beans used in many Asian desserts. They are available in most Asian grocery stores or online.
- **Sweetness:** Adjust the amount of sugar based on your preference. Some people prefer a sweeter soup, while others like it more subtle.
- **Texture:** If you prefer a smoother texture, you can use an immersion blender to blend the soup after cooking the beans. For a chunkier texture, only mash a portion of the beans.
- **Storage:** Leftover zenzai can be stored in the refrigerator for up to a week. Reheat gently on the stove over low heat. If the soup thickens too much upon cooling, you can add a bit of water to reach the desired consistency.

Zenzai is a comforting and satisfying dessert that's perfect for warming up on a cold day. Its combination of sweet red beans and chewy mochi makes it a beloved treat in Japanese cuisine. Enjoy this traditional sweet soup as a cozy treat or a special dessert for festive occasions.

Japanese Pumpkin Tempura

Ingredients:

For the Tempura:

- 1 small kabocha squash (about 1 lb/450 g)
- Vegetable oil, for frying

For the Tempura Batter:

- 1 cup (120 g) all-purpose flour
- 1/2 cup (60 g) cornstarch or potato starch
- 1 large egg
- 1 cup (240 ml) cold sparkling water (or very cold water)
- 1/2 teaspoon baking powder (optional, for extra crispiness)

For Serving:

- Tempura dipping sauce (Tentsuyu) or soy sauce
- Grated daikon radish (optional)
- Lemon wedges (optional)

Instructions:

1. **Prepare the Kabocha Squash:**
    - Wash the kabocha squash thoroughly. Cut it into thin, bite-sized wedges or slices, about 1/4 inch (6 mm) thick. You can leave the skin on for extra texture and color.
    - Remove the seeds and any fibrous strands from the inside of the squash.
2. **Prepare the Tempura Batter:**
    - In a large bowl, combine the flour, cornstarch (or potato starch), and baking powder (if using).
    - In a separate bowl, beat the egg and then add the cold sparkling water. Mix gently.
    - Add the egg mixture to the dry ingredients and stir lightly until just combined. The batter should be lumpy; do not overmix. Overmixing can make the batter dense.
3. **Heat the Oil:**
    - Heat vegetable oil in a deep fryer or large pot to 350-375°F (175-190°C). You'll need enough oil to fully submerge the tempura pieces.
4. **Coat and Fry the Kabocha:**
    - Lightly dust the kabocha slices with a bit of flour to help the batter adhere better.
    - Dip each kabocha slice into the tempura batter, allowing any excess batter to drip off.

- Carefully slide the battered kabocha slices into the hot oil. Fry in batches, without overcrowding, for about 2-3 minutes or until the tempura is golden brown and crispy.
- Use a slotted spoon or spider strainer to remove the tempura from the oil and drain on a paper towel-lined plate.

5. **Serve:**
    - Serve the hot tempura immediately with tempura dipping sauce (Tentsuyu) or soy sauce. You can also garnish with grated daikon radish and lemon wedges if desired.

Notes:

- **Kabocha Squash:** Kabocha squash has a sweet, nutty flavor and a rich texture. If kabocha is not available, you can substitute with other types of squash or pumpkin.
- **Batter Temperature:** Keeping the batter cold helps it to stay crisp during frying. Cold sparkling water also adds lightness to the batter.
- **Oil Temperature:** Make sure the oil is hot enough to create a crispy texture. If the oil is too cool, the tempura will absorb more oil and become greasy.
- **Serving:** Tempura is best enjoyed fresh and hot. If you need to reheat leftovers, do so in an oven or toaster oven to retain crispiness, rather than using a microwave.

Japanese Pumpkin Tempura is a wonderful way to enjoy the natural sweetness and rich flavor of kabocha squash. Its crispy exterior and tender interior make it a perfect snack or side dish for any meal.

Yakitori (Grilled Chicken Skewers)

Ingredients:

For the Yakitori Skewers:

- 1 lb (450 g) chicken thighs or chicken breast, boneless and skinless
- 1/2 cup (120 ml) soy sauce
- 1/4 cup (60 ml) mirin (sweet rice wine)
- 1/4 cup (60 ml) sake (Japanese rice wine)
- 2 tablespoons granulated sugar
- 2 tablespoons vegetable oil (for grilling)
- Bamboo skewers (soaked in water for 30 minutes to prevent burning)

Optional:

- Salt (for seasoning)
- Green onions, cut into 1-inch pieces
- Shishito peppers or other vegetables (if desired)

For the Yakitori Sauce (Tare):

- 1/2 cup (120 ml) soy sauce
- 1/4 cup (60 ml) mirin
- 1/4 cup (60 ml) sake
- 3 tablespoons granulated sugar

Instructions:

1. **Prepare the Chicken:**
   - Cut the chicken into bite-sized pieces, about 1 to 1.5 inches (2.5 to 4 cm) each. If using chicken thighs, you may want to remove any excess fat or skin.
   - If using green onions or other vegetables, cut them into similar-sized pieces.
2. **Make the Yakitori Sauce (Tare):**
   - In a small saucepan, combine soy sauce, mirin, sake, and sugar. Bring to a simmer over medium heat.
   - Stir until the sugar is dissolved and the sauce is slightly thickened, about 5-7 minutes.
   - Remove from heat and let cool. The sauce will continue to thicken as it cools.
3. **Assemble the Skewers:**
   - Thread the chicken pieces onto the soaked bamboo skewers, alternating with green onion pieces if using. You can also add vegetables to the skewers if desired.
4. **Grill the Yakitori:**

- Preheat a grill or grill pan over medium-high heat. Brush the grill grates with vegetable oil to prevent sticking.
- Place the skewers on the grill and cook for about 3-4 minutes per side, or until the chicken is cooked through and has grill marks. If using a grill pan, you may need to cook in batches.
- Brush the yakitori with the yakitori sauce during the last few minutes of grilling. This allows the sauce to caramelize and create a delicious glaze.

5. **Serve:**
   - Remove the skewers from the grill and season with a sprinkle of salt if desired.
   - Serve immediately with additional yakitori sauce on the side for dipping or drizzling.

Notes:

- **Chicken Parts:** Traditional yakitori often uses different parts of the chicken, such as thighs, breasts, or even liver. Feel free to experiment with different cuts based on your preference.
- **Sauce Variations:** You can adjust the sweetness and saltiness of the sauce by modifying the amount of sugar and soy sauce. For a slightly tangier version, you can add a splash of rice vinegar.
- **Grilling:** If using an outdoor grill, you may want to use indirect heat to prevent burning and ensure even cooking. For indoor grilling, a grill pan or broiler works well.
- **Serving Suggestions:** Yakitori can be served with steamed rice, pickled vegetables, or a simple salad. It also pairs well with a cold beer or a glass of sake.

Yakitori is a delicious and versatile dish that's perfect for both casual dinners and special gatherings. Its smoky, savory flavor and tender chicken make it a crowd-pleaser that brings a taste of Japan to your table. Enjoy grilling and savoring these flavorful chicken skewers!

Shirasu (Whitebait) Rice Bowl

Ingredients:

For the Rice Bowl:

- 2 cups (360 g) short-grain Japanese rice (such as sushi rice)
- 2 1/2 cups (600 ml) water (for cooking rice)
- 1 cup (150 g) shirasu (whitebait), fresh or dried
- 1 tablespoon soy sauce (optional, for seasoning shirasu)
- 2 tablespoons sesame seeds (optional, for garnish)
- 2-3 green onions, finely chopped (for garnish)
- Nori (seaweed) strips (for garnish)
- Pickled vegetables (for serving, optional)

For Serving:

- Soy sauce or ponzu sauce (for drizzling, optional)
- Pickled ginger (optional)

Instructions:

1. **Cook the Rice:**
   - Rinse the rice under cold water until the water runs clear to remove excess starch.
   - Combine the rinsed rice and 2 1/2 cups of water in a rice cooker or a heavy-bottomed pot.
   - Cook according to your rice cooker's instructions or, if using a pot, bring to a boil, then reduce the heat to low, cover, and simmer for 18-20 minutes. Let it sit covered for an additional 10 minutes before fluffing with a fork.
2. **Prepare the Shirasu:**
   - If using fresh shirasu, rinse them gently in cold water and drain. They can be used as-is or briefly blanched in boiling water for a few seconds if desired.
   - If using dried shirasu, they are usually ready to use. You can soak them briefly in water to rehydrate if needed, but they can also be served dry.
3. **Assemble the Rice Bowl:**
   - Divide the cooked rice into serving bowls.
   - Arrange the shirasu on top of the rice. If you like, you can lightly season the shirasu with soy sauce before placing them on the rice.
   - Garnish with sesame seeds, chopped green onions, and nori strips.
4. **Serve:**
   - Serve the Shirasu Don with additional soy sauce or ponzu sauce on the side for drizzling.
   - Accompany the dish with pickled vegetables and pickled ginger if desired.

Notes:

- **Fresh vs. Dried Shirasu:** Fresh shirasu are tender and have a milder taste, while dried shirasu are more concentrated in flavor and can be slightly crunchy. Both can be used depending on availability and preference.
- **Rice Cooking:** For best results, use short-grain or sushi rice for a stickier texture that complements the shirasu well.
- **Garnishes:** Feel free to add other garnishes like sliced radishes or a soft-boiled egg for extra flavor and texture.
- **Seasoning:** The shirasu don is traditionally enjoyed with minimal seasoning to let the natural flavor of the shirasu shine through. However, you can adjust the seasoning to taste.

Shirasu Don is a simple yet satisfying dish that highlights the delicate flavor of shirasu. It's perfect for a quick lunch or a light dinner, and it offers a taste of traditional Japanese cuisine. Enjoy this flavorful rice bowl as a delicious and easy-to-make meal!

Mentaiko Pasta

Ingredients:

- 8 oz (225 g) spaghetti
- 2 tablespoons butter
- 2 cloves garlic, minced
- 1/2 cup (120 ml) heavy cream
- 1/2 cup (120 ml) pasta cooking water (reserved)
- 1/2 cup (100 g) mentaiko (cod roe), removed from sacs
- 2 tablespoons soy sauce
- 1 tablespoon mirin (sweet rice wine)
- 1 tablespoon chopped fresh parsley or green onions (for garnish)
- Nori (seaweed) strips, for garnish (optional)
- 1 tablespoon sesame seeds (optional)

Instructions:

1. **Cook the Pasta:**
    - Bring a large pot of salted water to a boil. Add the spaghetti and cook according to package instructions until al dente. Reserve about 1/2 cup (120 ml) of the pasta cooking water before draining the pasta.
2. **Prepare the Sauce:**
    - While the pasta is cooking, melt the butter in a large skillet over medium heat.
    - Add the minced garlic and sauté until fragrant, about 1 minute. Be careful not to burn the garlic.
    - Reduce the heat to low and add the heavy cream. Stir to combine and let it heat through.
3. **Add Mentaiko:**
    - Remove the mentaiko from its sacs and add it to the skillet. Stir gently to mix with the cream, being careful not to break up the roe too much.
    - Add soy sauce and mirin to the skillet, stirring to combine. Adjust the seasoning to taste.
4. **Combine Pasta and Sauce:**
    - Add the drained spaghetti to the skillet, tossing to coat the pasta with the mentaiko sauce. If the sauce is too thick, add a little reserved pasta cooking water, a tablespoon at a time, until you reach the desired consistency.
5. **Serve:**
    - Divide the pasta among serving plates.
    - Garnish with chopped parsley or green onions, and optionally, nori strips and sesame seeds.
    - Serve immediately.

Notes:

- **Mentaiko:** Mentaiko is often available in Asian grocery stores or Japanese markets. If mentaiko is unavailable, you can use tarako (another type of cod roe) as a substitute.
- **Spice Level:** Mentaiko can range from mild to spicy. Adjust the amount of roe or add a pinch of red pepper flakes if you prefer a spicier dish.
- **Creaminess:** If you prefer a richer sauce, you can increase the amount of heavy cream. For a lighter version, use less cream or substitute with milk.
- **Garnishes:** Traditional garnishes include chopped fresh parsley or green onions. Nori strips and sesame seeds add additional flavor and texture.
- **Leftovers:** Mentaiko pasta is best enjoyed fresh. If you have leftovers, store them in an airtight container in the refrigerator for up to 1-2 days. Reheat gently on the stove, adding a splash of cream or pasta water if needed.

Mentaiko Pasta is a delicious fusion dish that brings together Italian pasta with Japanese flavors, offering a unique and satisfying meal. Its creamy texture and umami-rich sauce make it a favorite for both casual dinners and special occasions. Enjoy the rich taste of this comforting pasta dish!

Takoyaki Okonomiyaki

Ingredients:

For the Takoyaki:

- 1 cup (120 g) takoyaki flour (or use all-purpose flour with a pinch of baking powder)
- 1 large egg
- 1 cup (240 ml) dashi stock (or water)
- 1/2 cup (100 g) cooked octopus, chopped into small pieces
- 1/4 cup (30 g) pickled ginger, finely chopped
- 1/4 cup (30 g) green onions, chopped
- 1/4 cup (30 g) tempura scraps (tenkasu)
- 1/2 cup (60 g) shredded cheddar cheese (optional)

For the Okonomiyaki Batter:

- 1 cup (120 g) all-purpose flour
- 1/2 cup (120 ml) dashi stock (or water)
- 1 large egg
- 1 cup (70 g) shredded cabbage
- 1/4 cup (30 g) green onions, chopped
- 1/4 cup (30 g) cooked bacon or ham, chopped (optional)
- 1/4 cup (30 g) cooked shrimp or squid (optional)

For Toppings:

- Okonomiyaki sauce (store-bought or homemade)
- Japanese mayonnaise
- Aonori (dried seaweed flakes)
- Katsuobushi (dried bonito flakes)
- Pickled ginger (for garnish)
- Additional chopped green onions (for garnish)

Instructions:

1. **Prepare Takoyaki Batter:**
    - In a large bowl, mix the takoyaki flour, egg, and dashi stock until smooth.
    - Gently fold in the cooked octopus, pickled ginger, green onions, tempura scraps, and cheese (if using).
2. **Prepare Okonomiyaki Batter:**
    - In a separate bowl, whisk together the all-purpose flour, dashi stock, and egg until smooth.

- Stir in the shredded cabbage, green onions, bacon or ham, and shrimp or squid (if using).
3. **Cook Takoyaki Balls:**
   - Heat a takoyaki pan or a non-stick skillet over medium heat. Lightly grease the pan with oil.
   - Pour the takoyaki batter into the wells of the takoyaki pan, filling them about halfway. Cook for about 1-2 minutes, then use a skewer or chopsticks to turn the takoyaki balls so they cook evenly. Cook for another 1-2 minutes until golden brown and crispy. Remove from the pan and set aside.
4. **Cook Okonomiyaki:**
   - Heat a non-stick skillet or griddle over medium heat and lightly grease with oil.
   - Pour the okonomiyaki batter into the skillet, spreading it into a circle about 1/2 inch (1.5 cm) thick.
   - Place the cooked takoyaki balls on top of the okonomiyaki batter. Press them down slightly.
   - Cook for about 3-4 minutes, then flip carefully and cook for another 3-4 minutes on the other side, or until golden brown and cooked through.
5. **Serve:**
   - Transfer the Takoyaki Okonomiyaki to a serving plate.
   - Drizzle with okonomiyaki sauce and Japanese mayonnaise.
   - Sprinkle with aonori, katsuobushi, and additional chopped green onions.
   - Garnish with pickled ginger if desired.

Notes:

- **Takoyaki Flour:** Takoyaki flour is a specialized flour mix for making takoyaki. If unavailable, you can substitute with a mixture of all-purpose flour and a pinch of baking powder.
- **Cooking Equipment:** If you don't have a takoyaki pan, you can use a regular non-stick skillet or griddle to cook the takoyaki balls. Simply shape them into small balls and cook until golden and crispy.
- **Okonomiyaki Variations:** Feel free to customize the Okonomiyaki with additional ingredients such as mushrooms, corn, or other vegetables based on your preference.
- **Toppings:** The toppings are essential for authentic Okonomiyaki flavor. Adjust the amounts based on your taste and availability.

This Takoyaki Okonomiyaki fusion dish brings together the best of both worlds, combining the savory goodness of octopus balls with the rich, pancake-like flavors of Okonomiyaki. Enjoy this creative and delicious twist on classic Japanese street food!

Sukiyaki Beef Rolls

Ingredients:

For the Beef Rolls:

- 1/2 lb (225 g) thinly sliced beef (such as sirloin or ribeye)
- 1 small carrot, julienned
- 1/2 bell pepper, julienned
- 4-5 green onions, cut into 2-inch pieces
- 1 cup (70 g) shimeji mushrooms or enoki mushrooms (optional)
- Salt and pepper to taste
- 2 tablespoons vegetable oil

For the Sukiyaki Sauce:

- 1/4 cup (60 ml) soy sauce
- 1/4 cup (60 ml) mirin (sweet rice wine)
- 2 tablespoons sugar
- 2 tablespoons sake (Japanese rice wine)
- 1/2 cup (120 ml) dashi stock or water

For Garnish (optional):

- Chopped fresh parsley or green onions
- Sesame seeds

Instructions:

1. **Prepare the Ingredients:**
   - If using mushrooms, trim and clean them. For shimeji mushrooms, separate them into clusters. For enoki mushrooms, trim off the root end and separate into smaller bunches.
   - Cut the carrot, bell pepper, and green onions into thin strips.
2. **Prepare the Sukiyaki Sauce:**
   - In a small saucepan, combine soy sauce, mirin, sugar, sake, and dashi stock or water. Bring to a simmer over medium heat, stirring until the sugar is dissolved.
   - Reduce the heat and let the sauce simmer for about 5 minutes. Remove from heat and set aside.
3. **Assemble the Beef Rolls:**
   - Lay out the thinly sliced beef on a cutting board. Season lightly with salt and pepper.
   - Place a few pieces of carrot, bell pepper, green onions, and mushrooms (if using) at one end of each beef slice.

- Roll the beef around the vegetables, securing with toothpicks if needed.
4. **Cook the Beef Rolls:**
   - Heat vegetable oil in a large skillet over medium-high heat.
   - Add the beef rolls to the skillet and cook, turning occasionally, until the beef is browned and cooked through, about 3-4 minutes per side.
   - Remove the beef rolls from the skillet and set aside.
5. **Glaze with Sukiyaki Sauce:**
   - In the same skillet, pour in the prepared sukiyaki sauce and bring to a simmer.
   - Return the beef rolls to the skillet and simmer in the sauce for about 2-3 minutes, basting with the sauce to coat evenly. This will allow the flavors to meld and the sauce to thicken slightly.
6. **Serve:**
   - Transfer the beef rolls to a serving platter.
   - Garnish with chopped fresh parsley or green onions and a sprinkle of sesame seeds if desired.
   - Serve hot, either as an appetizer or with steamed rice as a main dish.

Notes:

- **Beef:** For best results, use very thinly sliced beef. If you can't find pre-sliced beef, you can freeze a piece of beef slightly to firm it up and slice it thinly yourself.
- **Vegetables:** Feel free to customize the filling with other vegetables like mushrooms, spinach, or bell peppers according to your preference.
- **Sukiyaki Sauce:** Adjust the sweetness and saltiness of the sauce to your taste. You can add more sugar or soy sauce if needed.
- **Cooking Tips:** Be gentle when rolling the beef to avoid tearing. Use toothpicks if necessary to help hold the rolls together while cooking.

Sukiyaki Beef Rolls offer a tasty and visually appealing way to enjoy the classic flavors of sukiyaki. This recipe provides a delightful combination of tender beef and flavorful vegetables, making it a perfect dish for any occasion. Enjoy your meal!

Goya Champuru (Bitter Melon Stir-Fry)

Ingredients:

- 1 medium bitter melon (goya), seeds removed and sliced thinly
- 1 block (14 oz or 400 g) firm tofu, drained and cubed
- 1/2 lb (225 g) pork belly or pork loin, thinly sliced (or substitute with chicken or beef)
- 1 onion, sliced
- 2 cloves garlic, minced
- 1 tablespoon vegetable oil
- 2 tablespoons soy sauce
- 1 tablespoon mirin (sweet rice wine)
- 1 tablespoon sake (Japanese rice wine)
- 1 tablespoon oyster sauce (optional)
- 2 eggs, lightly beaten
- Salt and pepper to taste
- 1/4 cup (30 g) dried bonito flakes (katsuobushi) or shredded cheddar cheese (optional, for garnish)
- 1-2 green onions, sliced (for garnish)

Instructions:

1. **Prepare the Bitter Melon:**
    - Cut the bitter melon in half lengthwise and scoop out the seeds using a spoon.
    - Slice the melon thinly. To reduce the bitterness, sprinkle the slices with a little salt and let them sit for about 10 minutes. Rinse well and pat dry with paper towels.
2. **Prepare the Tofu:**
    - Cut the tofu into bite-sized cubes. If using firm tofu, you may want to press it gently to remove excess moisture.
3. **Cook the Pork:**
    - Heat vegetable oil in a large skillet or wok over medium-high heat.
    - Add the sliced pork and cook until browned and cooked through, about 3-4 minutes. Remove from the skillet and set aside.
4. **Stir-Fry the Vegetables:**
    - In the same skillet, add a bit more oil if needed. Sauté the onion and garlic until fragrant and translucent, about 2 minutes.
    - Add the bitter melon slices and stir-fry for about 5-7 minutes, until they are tender but still slightly crisp. If you prefer a milder bitterness, cook a bit longer.
5. **Add Tofu and Pork:**
    - Add the cubed tofu and cooked pork back into the skillet. Stir to combine.
6. **Season the Dish:**
    - Pour in the soy sauce, mirin, sake, and oyster sauce (if using). Stir well to coat all the ingredients evenly.

- Cook for an additional 2-3 minutes, allowing the flavors to meld.

7. **Add Eggs:**
   - Push the ingredients to one side of the skillet. Pour the beaten eggs into the empty side and scramble until cooked through. Gently fold the scrambled eggs into the rest of the stir-fry.

8. **Serve:**
   - Season with salt and pepper to taste.
   - Transfer to a serving platter and garnish with green onions and, if desired, dried bonito flakes or shredded cheese.

Notes:

- **Bitter Melon:** Goya is known for its bitter taste. The salting method helps to reduce some of the bitterness, but the flavor is an integral part of the dish. Adjust the bitterness to your liking by cooking the melon longer if needed.
- **Pork:** Pork belly is traditional, but pork loin or chicken can be used as alternatives. For a vegetarian version, you can omit the meat or use a plant-based protein.
- **Tofu:** Firm tofu works best for this dish as it holds its shape well during cooking.
- **Seasoning:** Adjust the seasoning based on your taste preferences. The combination of soy sauce, mirin, and sake adds a balanced flavor, but you can tweak it as desired.
- **Garnishes:** Bonito flakes add an extra umami flavor, while shredded cheese can provide a different taste. Choose according to your preference or omit if not available.

Goya Champuru is a flavorful and nutritious dish that showcases the unique taste of bitter melon. Its combination of savory pork, tofu, and vegetables makes it a satisfying meal that is both delicious and healthful. Enjoy this taste of Okinawan cuisine!

Tempura Soba

Ingredients:

For the Tempura:

- 1/2 cup (60 g) all-purpose flour
- 1/4 cup (30 g) cornstarch
- 1/2 teaspoon baking powder
- 1/2 cup (120 ml) cold sparkling water (or ice water)
- 1/2 teaspoon salt
- 10-12 large shrimp, peeled and deveined
- 1 small sweet potato, peeled and thinly sliced
- 1 small zucchini, sliced into rounds
- 1/2 onion, thinly sliced into rings
- Vegetable oil, for frying

For the Soba Broth:

- 4 cups (960 ml) dashi stock (can be homemade or store-bought)
- 1/4 cup (60 ml) soy sauce
- 2 tablespoons mirin (sweet rice wine)
- 1 tablespoon sake (Japanese rice wine)
- 1 teaspoon sugar (optional)

For the Soba Noodles:

- 8 oz (225 g) soba noodles
- 2 green onions, thinly sliced
- 1/4 cup (10 g) dried nori (seaweed) strips (optional)
- Shichimi togarashi (seven-spice blend), for garnish (optional)

Instructions:

1. **Prepare the Tempura Batter:**
    - In a mixing bowl, combine the all-purpose flour, cornstarch, baking powder, and salt.
    - Add the cold sparkling water (or ice water) and gently mix until just combined. Do not overmix; it's okay if there are some lumps.
2. **Prepare the Tempura Ingredients:**
    - Heat vegetable oil in a deep skillet or frying pan to 350°F (180°C). You'll need enough oil to submerge the tempura ingredients.
    - Dip the shrimp and vegetables into the tempura batter, allowing any excess to drip off.

- Carefully place them into the hot oil. Fry in batches, making sure not to overcrowd the pan. Cook until the tempura is golden brown and crispy, about 2-3 minutes for shrimp and 3-4 minutes for vegetables.
- Remove from the oil and drain on paper towels. Keep warm.

3. **Prepare the Soba Broth:**
   - In a large saucepan, combine the dashi stock, soy sauce, mirin, and sake. Bring to a simmer over medium heat. If desired, add sugar to taste.
   - Simmer for about 5 minutes, then remove from heat.
4. **Cook the Soba Noodles:**
   - Cook the soba noodles according to the package instructions until just tender. Drain and rinse under cold water to stop the cooking process and remove excess starch.
5. **Assemble the Dish:**
   - Divide the cooked soba noodles among serving bowls.
   - Ladle the hot soba broth over the noodles.
   - Top with crispy tempura.
   - Garnish with sliced green onions, dried nori strips, and a sprinkle of shichimi togarashi if using.

Notes:

- **Tempura Batter:** The key to crispy tempura is using cold sparkling water and mixing the batter lightly. The batter should be lumpy and not too smooth.
- **Dashi Stock:** Dashi is a fundamental Japanese stock made from kombu (seaweed) and bonito flakes. You can use instant dashi powder for convenience if you don't have homemade dashi.
- **Serving:** Tempura is best enjoyed immediately while it's still crispy. If you need to hold it for a while, keep the tempura warm in a low oven, but be aware that it may lose some crispiness.
- **Noodles:** Soba noodles have a slightly nutty flavor and firm texture that pairs well with the broth and tempura. They are also a healthier alternative to other types of noodles.
- **Garnishes:** Customize the garnishes according to your taste. Green onions add freshness, while nori and shichimi togarashi add extra flavor and texture.

Tempura Soba is a classic Japanese dish that beautifully combines the flavors and textures of crispy tempura with savory soba noodles and broth. It's a comforting and delicious meal that's perfect for any occasion. Enjoy your Tempura Soba!

Katsu Sandwich

Ingredients:

For the Katsu:

- 2 boneless pork chops or chicken breasts (about 1/2 inch thick)
- 1/2 cup (60 g) all-purpose flour
- 1 large egg
- 1 cup (100 g) panko breadcrumbs
- Salt and pepper to taste
- Vegetable oil, for frying

For the Sandwich:

- 4 slices of soft white bread (such as shokupan or sandwich bread)
- 2 tablespoons tonkatsu sauce (store-bought or homemade)
- 1 tablespoon mayonnaise (optional)
- Shredded cabbage (optional)
- Pickles (optional, for added crunch)

For Homemade Tonkatsu Sauce (optional):

- 1/4 cup (60 ml) ketchup
- 2 tablespoons Worcestershire sauce
- 1 tablespoon soy sauce
- 1 tablespoon mirin (sweet rice wine)
- 1 tablespoon sugar

Instructions:

1. **Prepare the Katsu:**
    - If using pork chops, place them between two sheets of plastic wrap and pound them to an even thickness using a meat mallet. Season both sides with salt and pepper.
    - Set up a breading station: Place the flour, beaten egg, and panko breadcrumbs in separate shallow dishes.
    - Dredge each pork chop or chicken breast in the flour, shaking off excess. Dip into the beaten egg, then coat with panko breadcrumbs, pressing down gently to adhere.
2. **Fry the Katsu:**
    - Heat vegetable oil in a large skillet or frying pan over medium-high heat. You'll need enough oil to cover the bottom of the pan.

- Once the oil is hot, carefully place the breaded cutlets in the pan. Fry until golden brown and cooked through, about 4-5 minutes per side, depending on thickness.
- Remove from the skillet and drain on paper towels. Let cool slightly before slicing.

3. **Prepare the Tonkatsu Sauce (if making homemade):**
   - In a small bowl, combine ketchup, Worcestershire sauce, soy sauce, mirin, and sugar. Stir until the sugar is dissolved and the sauce is well combined.
4. **Assemble the Sandwich:**
   - Spread tonkatsu sauce on one side of each slice of bread. If using, spread mayonnaise on the other side of each slice.
   - Place a layer of shredded cabbage on two slices of bread (if using). Top with the cooked katsu cutlets. Add pickles if desired.
   - Place the remaining bread slices on top, sauce side down.
5. **Serve:**
   - Cut the sandwiches in half or into quarters if desired. Serve immediately, or wrap in parchment paper for a portable lunch.

Notes:

- **Tonkatsu Sauce:** Store-bought tonkatsu sauce is readily available and works well, but homemade sauce can add a personal touch.
- **Bread:** Soft white bread works best for a classic Katsu Sandwich, but you can use other types of bread if preferred.
- **Variations:** You can substitute the pork with chicken or even use a vegetarian option like a breaded and fried portobello mushroom.
- **Cabbage:** Adding shredded cabbage provides a crunchy texture and a fresh contrast to the rich, crispy katsu.
- **Pickles:** Japanese pickles or simple pickled cucumber slices can add extra crunch and flavor to the sandwich.

Katsu Sandwich is a delightful and satisfying meal that combines crispy, juicy katsu with the comforting texture of soft bread. It's perfect for a quick lunch or as a flavorful snack. Enjoy making and eating your delicious Katsu Sandwich!

Yakimeshi (Fried Rice)

Ingredients:

- 2 cups cooked rice (preferably cold or day-old)
- 1/2 cup (75 g) diced ham, cooked chicken, or shrimp (or a combination)
- 1/2 cup (75 g) frozen peas and carrots
- 2 green onions, chopped
- 2 cloves garlic, minced
- 1 small onion, finely chopped
- 2 large eggs, lightly beaten
- 2 tablespoons soy sauce
- 1 tablespoon mirin (sweet rice wine) (optional)
- 1 tablespoon vegetable oil
- Salt and pepper to taste
- Sesame seeds (for garnish, optional)
- Sliced green onions (for garnish, optional)

Instructions:

1. **Prepare the Ingredients:**
   - If using frozen peas and carrots, thaw them by placing them in a bowl of warm water or microwaving briefly. Drain well.
   - Make sure the rice is cold or at least cool. Freshly cooked rice tends to be too moist and can become mushy when stir-frying.
2. **Cook the Protein:**
   - Heat 1 tablespoon of vegetable oil in a large skillet or wok over medium-high heat.
   - Add the diced ham, chicken, or shrimp and cook until heated through and slightly crispy. Remove from the skillet and set aside.
3. **Cook the Vegetables:**
   - In the same skillet, add a little more oil if necessary. Sauté the chopped onion and garlic until they are translucent and fragrant, about 2-3 minutes.
   - Add the frozen peas and carrots and cook for an additional 2 minutes, until they are tender.
4. **Scramble the Eggs:**
   - Push the vegetables to one side of the skillet and pour the beaten eggs into the empty space. Scramble the eggs until fully cooked, then mix them with the vegetables.
5. **Stir-Fry the Rice:**
   - Add the cold rice to the skillet. Break up any clumps and stir-fry the rice with the vegetables and eggs for about 3-4 minutes until the rice is heated through and slightly crispy.

6. **Season the Rice:**
   - Pour the soy sauce and mirin (if using) over the rice. Stir well to ensure the rice is evenly coated with the seasoning. Adjust seasoning with salt and pepper to taste.
7. **Add the Protein:**
   - Return the cooked ham, chicken, or shrimp to the skillet. Mix well to combine with the rice.
8. **Serve:**
   - Transfer the yakimeshi to serving plates.
   - Garnish with sesame seeds and sliced green onions if desired.

Notes:

- **Rice:** Using day-old rice or chilled rice is ideal for fried rice dishes. It helps the rice grains stay separate and prevents the dish from becoming mushy.
- **Protein:** You can use any protein of your choice, such as beef, tofu, or even a mix of different meats. For a vegetarian version, omit the meat and add more vegetables.
- **Vegetables:** Customize the vegetable mix based on your preference or availability. Bell peppers, mushrooms, and corn can also be added.
- **Soy Sauce:** Adjust the amount of soy sauce based on your taste and dietary needs. Low-sodium soy sauce can be used if you prefer less salt.
- **Garnishes:** Sesame seeds and green onions add extra flavor and a touch of freshness to the dish.

Yakimeshi is a delicious, quick-to-make dish that's perfect for using up leftover rice and can be adapted to fit whatever ingredients you have on hand. Enjoy this easy and flavorful fried rice!

Miso Soup with Clams

Ingredients:

- 4 cups (960 ml) dashi stock (can be homemade or store-bought)
- 1/4 cup (60 g) white miso paste (adjust to taste)
- 1 lb (450 g) fresh clams (such as littleneck or Manila), scrubbed and rinsed
- 1/2 cup (100 g) tofu, cut into small cubes
- 2 green onions, thinly sliced
- 1 small piece of kombu (dried kelp), about 4 inches long (optional, for additional umami)
- 1-2 tablespoons sake (Japanese rice wine) (optional)
- 1 tablespoon soy sauce (optional, adjust to taste)
- 1 tablespoon mirin (sweet rice wine) (optional)
- Fresh cilantro or chopped scallions, for garnish (optional)

Instructions:

1. **Prepare the Dashi Stock:**
   - If using kombu, add it to a pot with 4 cups of water. Heat over medium heat and remove the kombu just before the water starts to boil.
   - Add dried bonito flakes (if using) to the pot and let it simmer for a few minutes. Strain the stock through a fine sieve to remove the flakes. You can also use instant dashi powder or store-bought dashi stock for convenience.
2. **Cook the Clams:**
   - Place the clams in a large bowl of cold water and let them soak for about 20 minutes to expel any sand. Rinse them thoroughly.
   - In a separate pot, bring a small amount of water to a boil and add the clams. Cook until the clams open, about 3-5 minutes. Discard any clams that do not open. Remove the clams from their shells and set aside, or leave them in their shells for presentation.
3. **Prepare the Miso Soup:**
   - Heat the dashi stock in a pot over medium heat. If using kombu, remove it once the stock is hot but not boiling.
   - In a small bowl, mix a few ladles of hot dashi with the miso paste to dissolve it, then return this mixture to the pot. Stir to combine. Avoid boiling the soup after adding the miso to prevent bitterness.
   - Add the tofu cubes and let them heat through in the miso soup.
4. **Combine Ingredients:**
   - Gently add the cooked clams to the miso soup and heat them through.
   - If desired, add sake, soy sauce, and mirin to the soup for additional depth of flavor. Adjust the seasoning to taste.
5. **Serve:**
   - Ladle the miso soup into bowls.

- Garnish with sliced green onions, fresh cilantro, or chopped scallions if desired.

Notes:

- **Clams:** Ensure the clams are thoroughly cleaned before cooking to avoid any grit in the soup. Soaking them helps with this process.
- **Miso Paste:** Adjust the amount of miso paste based on your taste preference. White miso paste is milder and sweeter, while red miso paste is stronger and saltier.
- **Tofu:** Firm tofu works best in miso soup as it holds its shape well. Silken tofu can be used but may break apart more easily.
- **Kombu and Bonito Flakes:** Adding kombu and bonito flakes enhances the umami flavor of the dashi stock. If you prefer a quicker version, you can skip these and use instant dashi powder or store-bought dashi.
- **Garnishes:** Fresh herbs like cilantro or scallions add a nice touch of flavor and color.

Miso Soup with Clams is a delightful and nourishing soup that's easy to prepare. The combination of rich miso broth and tender clams makes for a comforting and flavorful dish. Enjoy your homemade miso soup!

Kake Udon

Ingredients:

- **For the Broth:**
    - 4 cups (960 ml) dashi stock (homemade or store-bought)
    - 1/4 cup (60 ml) soy sauce
    - 2 tablespoons mirin (sweet rice wine)
    - 1 tablespoon sake (Japanese rice wine) (optional)
    - 1 tablespoon sugar (optional, adjust to taste)
- **For the Udon:**
    - 8 oz (225 g) udon noodles (fresh or frozen)
- **Garnishes:**
    - 2 green onions, thinly sliced
    - 1/2 cup (50 g) sliced mushrooms (shiitake, enoki, or other varieties, optional)
    - 1 sheet nori (seaweed), cut into thin strips (optional)
    - Tempura flakes (tenkasu), for added crunch (optional)
    - Sesame seeds (optional)
    - Pickled ginger (optional)

Instructions:

1. **Prepare the Broth:**
    - In a large saucepan, combine the dashi stock, soy sauce, mirin, and sake (if using). Bring to a simmer over medium heat.
    - Taste the broth and adjust the seasoning with sugar if needed, or add a bit more soy sauce if a stronger flavor is desired.
    - Keep the broth warm over low heat.
2. **Cook the Udon Noodles:**
    - Cook the udon noodles according to the package instructions. If using fresh udon, this usually takes about 2-3 minutes. If using frozen or dried udon, follow the specific instructions provided.
    - Drain the noodles and rinse them under cold water to remove excess starch. This helps keep the noodles from becoming sticky.
3. **Assemble the Dish:**
    - Divide the cooked udon noodles among serving bowls.
    - Ladle the hot broth over the noodles.
4. **Add Garnishes:**
    - Top the soup with sliced green onions, mushrooms (if using), and any other desired garnishes like nori strips, tempura flakes, sesame seeds, or pickled ginger.
5. **Serve:**

- Serve the kake udon immediately while hot. Enjoy the comforting combination of udon noodles and savory broth!

Notes:

- **Dashi Stock:** For a quicker version, you can use instant dashi powder or store-bought dashi stock. Homemade dashi made from kombu and bonito flakes is traditional and adds a rich umami flavor.
- **Noodles:** Fresh or frozen udon noodles are best for this dish, but dried udon can also be used if that's what you have on hand. Just be sure to follow the cooking instructions on the package.
- **Garnishes:** Customize the garnishes based on your preferences or what you have available. Mushrooms add extra umami, while nori and tempura flakes offer additional textures and flavors.
- **Broth:** Adjust the broth seasoning to your taste. If you prefer a milder flavor, reduce the soy sauce or add more mirin.

Kake Udon is a classic, easy-to-make noodle soup that highlights the comforting and simple flavors of Japanese cuisine. Enjoy this warm and satisfying dish on a chilly day or whenever you need a quick and delicious meal!

Korean BBQ Beef

Ingredients:

- **For the Marinade:**
    - 1/4 cup (60 ml) soy sauce
    - 2 tablespoons brown sugar
    - 1 tablespoon honey
    - 1 tablespoon sesame oil
    - 3 cloves garlic, minced
    - 1-inch piece of ginger, grated
    - 2 tablespoons rice wine or sake
    - 1 tablespoon gochujang (Korean red chili paste) (optional, for added spice)
    - 1/2 teaspoon black pepper
    - 1/2 pear, grated or pureed (for tenderizing the meat) (or use an apple as an alternative)
    - 2 green onions, chopped
- **For the Beef:**
    - 1 lb (450 g) beef sirloin or ribeye, thinly sliced against the grain (freeze the beef slightly for easier slicing)
- **To Serve:**
    - Cooked rice
    - Lettuce leaves (for wrapping)
    - Kimchi (optional)
    - Sliced cucumbers or pickled radishes

Instructions:

1. **Prepare the Marinade:**
    - In a large bowl, combine soy sauce, brown sugar, honey, sesame oil, minced garlic, grated ginger, rice wine or sake, gochujang (if using), black pepper, and grated pear or apple. Mix well until the sugar is dissolved.
2. **Marinate the Beef:**
    - Add the thinly sliced beef to the marinade and toss to coat thoroughly.
    - Cover and refrigerate for at least 30 minutes, preferably 2-4 hours, or overnight for best flavor.
3. **Cook the Beef:**
    - **Grilling:** Preheat a grill or grill pan over medium-high heat. Grill the marinated beef slices for 2-3 minutes per side, or until cooked through and slightly charred.
    - **Pan-Cooking:** Heat a large skillet or wok over medium-high heat. Add a small amount of oil if needed. Add the marinated beef in a single layer and cook for 2-3 minutes per side, or until cooked through and slightly caramelized. You may need to cook in batches to avoid overcrowding the pan.

4. **Serve:**
   - Serve the Korean BBQ beef hot over cooked rice.
   - Accompany with lettuce leaves for wrapping, kimchi, and sliced cucumbers or pickled radishes if desired.

Notes:

- **Beef:** Thinly slicing the beef against the grain ensures tenderness. Freezing the beef slightly before slicing makes it easier to cut thin slices.
- **Marinade:** The pear or apple in the marinade helps tenderize the meat and adds a subtle sweetness. If you don't have a pear or apple, you can skip it, but it adds a nice flavor and texture.
- **Gochujang:** This ingredient adds a touch of spice and umami. If you prefer a milder version, you can omit it or use less.
- **Cooking Methods:** For a more authentic Korean BBQ experience, you can use a charcoal grill or tabletop grill if available. However, a stovetop grill pan or skillet works well for home cooking.

Korean BBQ Beef (Bulgogi) is a delicious and versatile dish that's perfect for any occasion. Its rich, savory flavors and tender beef make it a favorite at Korean restaurants and a great choice for homemade meals. Enjoy your Korean BBQ Beef!

Japanese Style Omelette (Tamagoyaki)

Ingredients:

- 4 large eggs
- 2 tablespoons soy sauce
- 1 tablespoon mirin (sweet rice wine)
- 1 tablespoon sugar
- 1 tablespoon vegetable oil or cooking oil
- 1/2 teaspoon dashi powder (optional, for extra umami flavor)
- Salt, to taste

Equipment:

- Rectangular tamagoyaki pan or a small non-stick skillet (about 6x8 inches)
- Chopsticks or a spatula
- Paper towels (for oiling the pan)

Instructions:

1. **Prepare the Egg Mixture:**
    - In a bowl, whisk the eggs until well combined and slightly frothy.
    - Add the soy sauce, mirin, sugar, and dashi powder (if using). Mix well until the sugar is dissolved. Adjust seasoning with salt if needed.
2. **Heat the Pan:**
    - Heat the rectangular tamagoyaki pan over medium heat. Lightly oil the pan with a paper towel dipped in vegetable oil, making sure to coat the entire surface. You may need to re-oil between batches.
3. **Cook the Tamagoyaki:**
    - Pour a small amount of the egg mixture (about 1/4 cup) into the pan, tilting the pan to spread the egg evenly. Allow it to cook until the edges are set but the surface is still slightly wet.
4. **Roll the Omelette:**
    - Once the egg is set, use chopsticks or a spatula to carefully roll the egg from one end of the pan to the other. Leave the rolled omelette in the pan and push it to one side.
    - Lightly oil the empty side of the pan, then pour another small amount of egg mixture into the pan, lifting the rolled omelette to let the new egg mixture flow underneath it.
    - Cook until the new layer is set but still slightly wet, then roll the omelette over the new layer.
    - Repeat this process, adding more egg mixture and rolling, until all the egg mixture is used and you have a layered omelette.

5. **Shape and Slice:**
   - Once the tamagoyaki is cooked through and has a nice golden color, remove it from the pan and let it cool slightly on a cutting board.
   - Slice the tamagoyaki into bite-sized pieces or desired portions.
6. **Serve:**
   - Serve the tamagoyaki warm or at room temperature, as part of a Japanese meal or in a bento box.

Notes:

- **Pan:** A rectangular tamagoyaki pan is ideal for making tamagoyaki, but a small non-stick skillet can be used if a rectangular pan is not available. The shape of the pan helps create the traditional rolled appearance.
- **Oil:** Ensure the pan is well-oiled to prevent sticking. Use a paper towel to spread a thin layer of oil evenly.
- **Rolling Technique:** Rolling the omelette may take some practice. Be gentle and try to keep the rolls tight for even layers.
- **Dashi Powder:** Adding dashi powder enhances the umami flavor but can be omitted if not available.

Tamagoyaki is a versatile and delicious dish that adds a touch of Japanese flavor to any meal. Its delicate sweetness and savory notes make it a favorite for many. Enjoy making and eating your tamagoyaki!

Saba Misoni (Miso Braised Mackerel)

Ingredients:

- 2 mackerel fillets (about 6-8 oz or 170-225 g each), boned and skinned
- 1 tablespoon vegetable oil
- 1/2 cup (120 ml) water
- 1/4 cup (60 ml) sake (Japanese rice wine)
- 1/4 cup (60 ml) mirin (sweet rice wine)
- 1/4 cup (60 ml) soy sauce
- 3 tablespoons miso paste (white or red)
- 2 tablespoons sugar
- 1 tablespoon rice vinegar (optional, for a touch of acidity)
- 2 green onions, sliced (for garnish)
- 1 tablespoon sesame seeds (for garnish, optional)

Instructions:

1. **Prepare the Mackerel:**
   - Rinse the mackerel fillets under cold water and pat them dry with paper towels. If you prefer, you can cut the fillets into smaller pieces for easier serving.
2. **Prepare the Sauce:**
   - In a medium bowl, whisk together the water, sake, mirin, soy sauce, miso paste, sugar, and rice vinegar (if using) until the miso and sugar are fully dissolved and the mixture is smooth.
3. **Cook the Mackerel:**
   - Heat the vegetable oil in a large skillet or saucepan over medium heat.
   - Add the mackerel fillets to the pan, skin-side down, and cook for about 2-3 minutes, or until the skin is lightly browned and crispy.
4. **Add the Sauce:**
   - Pour the prepared sauce over the mackerel fillets. The sauce should just cover the fish. If needed, add a bit more water to ensure the fillets are mostly submerged.
5. **Simmer:**
   - Bring the sauce to a gentle simmer, then reduce the heat to low. Cover the pan and let it simmer for about 15-20 minutes, or until the mackerel is cooked through and tender. Baste the fish with the sauce occasionally.
6. **Reduce the Sauce (Optional):**
   - If you prefer a thicker sauce, you can remove the mackerel from the pan once it's cooked and continue to simmer the sauce uncovered until it thickens to your liking.
7. **Serve:**
   - Transfer the mackerel fillets to a serving dish and spoon the sauce over the top.

- Garnish with sliced green onions and sesame seeds if desired.
8. **Accompany:**
    - Serve the Saba Misoni with steamed rice and a side of vegetables or pickles for a complete meal.

Notes:

- **Mackerel:** If fresh mackerel is not available, you can use frozen fillets. Just make sure to thaw them completely and pat them dry before cooking.
- **Miso Paste:** White miso paste is milder and sweeter, while red miso paste has a stronger, saltier flavor. You can adjust the type of miso paste based on your taste preference.
- **Cooking Time:** Cooking time may vary based on the thickness of the mackerel fillets. Ensure the fish is fully cooked and flakes easily with a fork.
- **Rice Vinegar:** Adding rice vinegar balances the sweetness of the sauce. If you prefer a sweeter sauce, you can omit it.

Saba Misoni is a flavorful and satisfying dish that showcases the umami richness of miso and the delicate taste of mackerel. Enjoy this traditional Japanese comfort food as part of a home-cooked meal!

Wasabi Mashed Potatoes

Ingredients:

- 2 lbs (900 g) Yukon Gold or Russet potatoes, peeled and cut into chunks
- 4 tablespoons unsalted butter
- 1/2 cup (120 ml) milk or heavy cream (adjust for desired creaminess)
- 2-3 tablespoons wasabi paste (adjust to taste)
- Salt, to taste
- Black pepper, to taste
- Chives or green onions, chopped (for garnish, optional)

Instructions:

1. **Cook the Potatoes:**
   - Place the peeled and cut potatoes in a large pot. Cover with cold water and add a generous pinch of salt.
   - Bring to a boil over medium-high heat, then reduce the heat to a simmer. Cook the potatoes for 15-20 minutes, or until tender and easily pierced with a fork.
2. **Drain and Mash:**
   - Drain the cooked potatoes and return them to the pot or a large mixing bowl.
   - Mash the potatoes using a potato masher or a ricer until smooth. For extra creaminess, you can use a hand mixer or stand mixer.
3. **Add Butter and Milk:**
   - While the potatoes are still hot, add the butter and mix until melted and fully incorporated.
   - Gradually add the milk or heavy cream, mixing until the potatoes reach your desired consistency. Adjust the amount of milk or cream based on how creamy you like your mashed potatoes.
4. **Incorporate Wasabi:**
   - Stir in the wasabi paste. Start with 2 tablespoons and taste, adding more if you prefer a stronger wasabi flavor. Mix thoroughly.
5. **Season and Serve:**
   - Season the mashed potatoes with salt and black pepper to taste.
   - Transfer to a serving dish and garnish with chopped chives or green onions if desired.

Notes:

- **Wasabi Paste:** Adjust the amount of wasabi paste to your taste. Wasabi can be quite strong, so start with a smaller amount and increase as needed.
- **Creaminess:** For even richer potatoes, you can use heavy cream instead of milk and add an extra tablespoon of butter.

- **Potatoes:** Yukon Gold potatoes are slightly buttery and creamy, making them ideal for mashed potatoes. Russet potatoes are also a good choice and can be fluffier.
- **Texture:** For a smoother texture, consider using a potato ricer. If you prefer a chunkier texture, a masher will work just fine.

Wasabi Mashed Potatoes are a delightful and surprising twist on a classic side dish. The wasabi adds a flavorful zing that elevates the mashed potatoes and complements a wide range of main courses. Enjoy this bold and creamy side dish with your favorite meals!

Nasu Dengaku (Miso Grilled Eggplant)

Ingredients:

- 2 medium eggplants (Japanese eggplants or globe eggplants)
- 2 tablespoons vegetable oil
- 1/4 cup (60 ml) white miso paste
- 2 tablespoons mirin (sweet rice wine)
- 1 tablespoon sake (Japanese rice wine)
- 2 tablespoons sugar
- 1 tablespoon soy sauce
- 1 teaspoon sesame seeds (optional, for garnish)
- 2 green onions, sliced (optional, for garnish)

Instructions:

1. **Prepare the Eggplants:**
    - Wash and cut the eggplants in half lengthwise. Score the flesh in a crisscross pattern, making shallow cuts. This helps the miso glaze penetrate and caramelize better.
2. **Preheat the Grill or Broiler:**
    - Preheat your grill to medium-high heat or set your oven's broiler to high.
3. **Prepare the Miso Glaze:**
    - In a small saucepan, combine the miso paste, mirin, sake, sugar, and soy sauce. Cook over medium heat, stirring constantly, until the sugar dissolves and the mixture becomes smooth and slightly thickened. Remove from heat and set aside.
4. **Grill or Broil the Eggplants:**
    - Brush the cut sides of the eggplants with vegetable oil.
    - Place the eggplants cut-side down on the grill or under the broiler. Grill or broil for about 4-5 minutes, or until the cut sides are charred and the eggplants are tender.
5. **Apply the Miso Glaze:**
    - Turn the eggplants cut-side up. Brush the miso glaze generously over the cut sides of the eggplants.
    - Return the eggplants to the grill or broiler and cook for an additional 3-5 minutes, or until the miso glaze is bubbly and caramelized. Watch closely to avoid burning.
6. **Garnish and Serve:**
    - Remove the eggplants from the grill or broiler and transfer to a serving platter.
    - Garnish with sesame seeds and sliced green onions if desired.
    - Serve warm.

Notes:

- **Miso Paste:** White miso is commonly used for a milder, sweeter glaze, but you can use red miso for a stronger, more savory flavor.
- **Grilling vs. Broiling:** If grilling, you can also use indirect heat to ensure the eggplants cook through without burning the glaze.
- **Eggplant Preparation:** Scoring the eggplant flesh helps the miso glaze penetrate and caramelize better.
- **Glaze Consistency:** If the glaze thickens too much, you can thin it with a little water or additional mirin.

Nasu Dengaku is a delicious way to enjoy eggplant with the rich umami flavor of miso. The caramelized glaze adds a lovely contrast to the tender, smoky eggplant. Enjoy this dish as a tasty appetizer, side dish, or part of a Japanese-themed meal!

Shiro Ebi (White Shrimp) Tempura

Ingredients:

- **For the Tempura:**
    - 12-15 shiro ebi (white shrimp), peeled and deveined, tails left on
    - 1 cup (120 g) all-purpose flour
    - 1/2 cup (60 g) cornstarch
    - 1 cup (240 ml) cold sparkling water (or ice-cold water)
    - 1 large egg, lightly beaten
    - Vegetable oil (for deep frying)
- **For the Tempura Dipping Sauce (Tentsuyu):**
    - 1/2 cup (120 ml) dashi broth (or water)
    - 1/4 cup (60 ml) soy sauce
    - 2 tablespoons mirin (sweet rice wine)
    - 1 tablespoon sugar (optional, adjust to taste)
- **Optional Garnishes:**
    - Grated daikon radish
    - Lemon wedges
    - Finely sliced green onions

Instructions:

1. **Prepare the Shrimp:**
    - If not already done, peel and devein the white shrimp, leaving the tails intact. Pat the shrimp dry with paper towels to remove excess moisture.
2. **Prepare the Tempura Batter:**
    - In a large bowl, sift together the flour and cornstarch.
    - In a separate bowl, mix the cold sparkling water (or ice-cold water) with the beaten egg.
    - Gently fold the wet ingredients into the dry ingredients, mixing until just combined. The batter should be lumpy; avoid overmixing to keep the tempura light and crispy.
3. **Prepare the Tempura Dipping Sauce (Tentsuyu):**
    - In a small saucepan, combine the dashi broth, soy sauce, mirin, and sugar (if using).
    - Heat the mixture over medium heat until it just begins to simmer. Remove from heat and let it cool to room temperature.
4. **Heat the Oil:**
    - In a deep pot or fryer, heat vegetable oil to 350°F (175°C). You need enough oil to fully submerge the shrimp.
5. **Fry the Tempura:**
    - Dip each shrimp into the tempura batter, allowing excess batter to drip off.

- Carefully slide the battered shrimp into the hot oil. Fry in batches to avoid overcrowding the pot.
- Fry for about 2-3 minutes, or until the tempura is golden brown and crispy. Use a slotted spoon to transfer the cooked shrimp to a plate lined with paper towels to drain excess oil.

6. **Serve:**
   - Arrange the tempura shrimp on a serving platter.
   - Serve with tempura dipping sauce (tentsuyu) on the side, along with optional garnishes like grated daikon radish, lemon wedges, and finely sliced green onions.

Notes:

- **Shrimp:** Shiro ebi are small, sweet white shrimp typically found in Japanese cuisine. If unavailable, you can use other small shrimp varieties.
- **Batter:** Cold sparkling water (or ice-cold water) helps create a light, crispy batter. If you don't have sparkling water, ice-cold still water can be used.
- **Oil Temperature:** Maintaining the correct oil temperature is crucial for crispy tempura. Use a thermometer to monitor the temperature and avoid overcrowding the pot to ensure even frying.
- **Serving:** Tempura is best served immediately after frying while the coating is still crispy.

Shiro Ebi Tempura showcases the delicate sweetness of white shrimp with a light and crispy batter, making it a delightful addition to any meal. Enjoy this elegant dish as part of a Japanese meal or as a special treat!

www.ingramcontent.com/pod-product-compliance
Lightning Source LLC
LaVergne TN
LVHW081557060526
838201LV00054B/1928